Shanti Parav

Des Raj Kali is an acclaimed Punjabi Dalit writer, historian and columnist. His primary areas of interest are the Ghadar movement, Dalit issues, Punjabi literature, myth and culture. He has published fourteen books; of them three are anthologies of short stories: *Kath-Kali* (1996), *Fakiri* (2006), and *Yahaan Chai Achhi Nahi Banti* (The Tea Isn't Good Here, 2015); and six are novels, with his first one, *Parneshwari* (2008), named after a peasant goddess, *Antaheen* (2008), *Pratham Pauran* (2009), *Shanti Parav* (2009), *Shehr Vich Saan Hon Da Matlabb* (What it Means to Be a Bull in the City, 2018), and *Tasihey Kade Buddhe Nahi Honde* (Sorrows Never Age, 2019). Kali has also authored four books of historical research on the Ghadar Party, a revolutionary organisation founded in America in 1913 to free India from British imperialism. As a journalist and columnist, he has written numerous essays on Punjabi society and culture. He also edits and runs a literary quarterly called *Lakeer*.

Neeti Singh is a poet, an accomplished translator, and Associate Professor of English with the Maharaja Sayajirao University in Baroda. Her research interests straddle Culture Studies, Bhakti/mystic poetry and Indian literatures in English. She has published over twenty-five research papers, and three books till date: *The Serpent of Slumber* (1995), a book of poems, followed by *Bhakti Poetry in Medieval India: Its Inception, Cultural Encounters and Impact with Reference to the Works of Kabir and Nanak* (2002), and a translation of *Bhai Jaita's Sri Gur Katha* (2015), a seventeenth-century epic of significant relevance to Sikh history and Bhakti poetics.

Manmohan, an Indian Police Service (IPS) officer, is a poet, writer, scholar, critic and translator of renown of Punjabi language and literature. His debut novel *Nirvaan* won the Sahitya Akademi Award in 2013.

Shanti Parav

Treatise on Peace

DES RAJ KALI

Translated from the original Punjabi by

NEETI SINGH

Orient BlackSwan

SHANTI PARAV: TREATISE ON PEACE

ORIENT BLACKSWAN PRIVATE LIMITED

Registered Office
3-6-752 Himayatnagar, Hyderabad 500 029, Telangana, India
e-mail: centraloffice@orientblackswan.com

Other Offices
Bengaluru, Bhopal, Chennai, Guwahati,
Hyderabad, Jaipur, Kolkata, Lucknow, Mumbai,
New Delhi, Noida, Patna, Visakhapatnam

Originally published in Punjabi as *Shanti Parav*
(Jalandhar: Deepak Publishers, 2009).

First published by Orient Blackswan Private Limited 2020

ISBN 978-93-5287-928-1

031362

Typeset in
Charis SIL 10/13
by Le Studio Graphique, Gurgaon 122 007

Printed in India at
Akash Press, Delhi

Published by
Orient Blackswan Private Limited
3-6-752 Himayatnagar, Hyderabad 500 029, Telangana, India
e-mail: info@orientblackswan.com

For my father Sardar Sohan Singh
and
for Professor Raj Kumar Hans

Contents

Publisher's acknowledgements

For granting permission to use copyrighted material in this volume, the publishers thank the following individuals and organisations:

Des Raj Kali, and Deepak Publishers, Jalandhar, for permission to translate Kali's novel *Shanti Parav*, originally published in Punjabi in 2009 by Deepak Publishers, Jalandhar.

Professor Linda Hess, for her translation of Kabir, *Sabda* 53, originally published in *The Bijak of Kabir* (Motilal Banarsidass, Delhi, 1986).

Mohan Kakanadan, Director, Gateway LitFest, for 'Writings from the Soil of Wounds: A Mulaquat with Des Raj Kali', originally published as 'Desraj Kali: Meditations on the Roots, Soil and Soul of Writing' on gatewaylitfest.com, 12 September 2017.

Acknowledgements

If you can see that tree
you'll be free
from age and death.
The tree is a whole world.

—Kabir*

That is how *Shanti Parav*, the anti-novel, has come to me. Like a 'tree' that embodies a truth and humbly proffers it to the whole world. Through the enterprise of translation and through engagement with both the novel and the novelist, I have grown in spirit and scholarship like a time-traveller, or a gypsy artist. Thank you Kali, for writing this.

And Professor Rajkumar Hans, for declaring at the 2014 October conference in Universite Paul-Valery, Montpellier, France: 'I know just the right person who will translate this!' You had just read in English a paper on Kali's novel *Shanti Parav*, and were defending your ground because the novel was in Punjabi. That gesture of yours is now history! I must thank the hosts of that seminar, Professor Nicole Thiara and Professor Judith Misrahi-Barak, for provoking it; and for their patronage and sustained initiatives which have launched many a deserving author and publisher, and brought to the fore several texts of literary worth from the Dalit grassroots. Des Raj Kali is a voice to reckon with.

Gratitude is due to Dr Manmohan for agreeing to grace this translation enterprise with an Introduction. And to Vidya Rao,

*Linda Hess and Shukdeo Singh, trans. *The Bijak of Kabir, Sabda* 53 (Delhi: Motilal Banarsidass, 1986), 58.

Moyna Mazumdar and the entire Orient BlackSwan team, for giving shape to this book. To my dear friend and colleague Professor Susan Bhatt, who was my first reader and sounding board, a warm thank you. To Professor Sudha Pandya, Professor Hitesh Raviya, Professor Sachin Ketkar, friends and colleagues of the Department of English, Maharaja Sayajirao University of Baroda, for their encouragement and support.

To father, who has been my severest friend and critic. His interventions have made this translation so much sharper and spot on. To mother, who was my first guide and teacher, I owe my familiarity with the Punjabi Gurmukhi. To her I owe most the Punjabiyat that runs in my bones!

And then there is Amrita. Thank you, poppet, for your unstinting faith and support. For putting up with me through long hours of silence (and sometimes no food), as I worked...sowing words piecemeal at odd hours into the laptop.

Neeti Singh

Shanti Parav: A post-modern Dalit narrative

Des Raj Kali, an established Punjabi writer, journalist and social thinker, brings with him in his writings a wealth of indigenous history, ethnographic detail and cultural traditions from the heartland of West Punjab. Born in Mithapur village, Jalandhar district, in a family of tanners, Kali grew up in the cradle of poverty and intense struggle, softened, however, by the benign presence of *pirs-fakirs* and an atmosphere of intimate association with mystic lore, myth and literature, to which he had access through the songs and stories passed down to him by his father, his uncles and his extended family.

'From carrying carcasses to creating characters' is how a newspaper headline in *The Times of India*, January 2016, describes Des Raj Kali, who has to his credit three collections of short stories: *Kath-Kali, Fakiri* and *Yahaan Chai Achhi Nahi Banti*, four books on the history of the Ghadar movement, and six novels: *Parneshwari, Antaheen, Pratham Pauran, Shanti Parav, Shehr Vich Saan Hon Da Matlabb*, which took him several years to complete, and his latest, *Tasihey Kade Buddhe Nahi Honde.* In terms of their length, one could categorise them as novellas, but if one perceives them in terms of their thematic content and polyphonic subjectivity, all these narratives can be placed in the genre of the novel. *Shehr Vich Saan Hon Da Matlabb,* in Kali's words, is about

> the Bull, which symbolises economy and the very deep impact it has on people. From [the] 90s until now, finance capital has enslaved us...has had its bearings on our psychology and the way we live. It has caused an atmosphere of uncertainty, insecurity and alienation. It has changed people's inherent perceptions and even religious beliefs.*

Most of Kali's characters are Dalits from the Doaba region of Punjab, whose issues figure prominently in his novels. One of the three old men in the 'under-text' of *Shanti Parav*, 'PbhagMull Pagal', for instance, is a real-life character from the Valmiki community. Bhagmal, who passed away a few years ago, was the secretary of the Scheduled Castes Federation formed by Babasaheb Ambedkar. I remember Kali once telling me about how he would visit Bhagmal and yet another character from real life, the Comrade. Kali spent much time and money on them both, buying them drinks or taking them to the doctor just to ensure that they were comfortable as they warmed up to him and shared with him significant details of their lives from memory.

Thus, on the one hand is Kali's experience of life from the grassroots of Dalit reality, and on the other is his uncanny insight and grasp of the socio-political history of Punjab as also its indigenous literatures, Indology and its Vedic texts. This uncanny gift that enables Kali to link structures of state, power and ideology with their reception by and impact on the collective psyche and their consequent seepage into the lives of ordinary people lends a sharp perspective, intellectual scope and a genius to his writing. A considerable wealth of detail and material that fills Kali's fictional world is a reflection of life as he has lived it and known it. To know more about the author's craft and creative context, see 'Writings from the soil of wounds: A *mulaquat* with Des Raj Kali' at the end of this volume.

As a writer, Kali functions ideologically from the context and standpoint of a Dalit/subaltern consciousness in all his works. He does not write for the sake of pleasure or to impress others by mere storytelling; rather, he speaks for those who have been compelled to keep silent for centuries. His characters and narratives present the bitter and crude realities of their sad and subordinate lives. Kali writes not with the pen but with molten iron, which pierces the hearts and minds of his readers. This is what gives his writing its raw, subversive power.

With all these narratives, Kali has created a convention of a specific kind of readership which does not read a text in the traditional sense, but reads between the lines. On reading his work the reader is left feeling disturbed or angry over unjust, discriminatory structures and exploitative apparatuses (in the language of Althusser) of societies and dominant, hegemonic centres of power. His narratives also draw deeply from myth and history wherein contexts of the past, present and future are textured and presented in such a way that the reader is compelled to move within the thick, complex tapestries of the life-worlds of the subaltern and the socially marginalised. Through these non-traditional narratives, Kali has been able to draw the attention of the Punjabi literary world.

Shanti Parav begins with the author's preface, 'Novel di gal' [About the novel], in which Kali explains his experimentation with the text as a genre and how he has used the subtext of the *Mahabharata*, both as a metaphor and as a point of departure with which to structure his own narrative. He says,

> This twelfth parav of the *Mahabharata* is of extreme importance as even today, we can see recurrent manifestations of its line of thought—it is an ideology that has continuously reproduced itself. It is a means to entering the folds of our *raj tantar*. It is a pathway to an understanding of the theology of our *Hakkam Pirs*. (p. xxiii of this volume)

Shanti Parav is a political narrative which introduces readers to and makes them aware of the complex and conflicting dynamics underlying contemporary Indian social and political realities. Kali's sharp language laced with puns and irony, his style, his vision, his Dalit/subaltern perspective and aesthetics attract and impress upon the reader to engage with his narrative. This slim yet compelling work, which runs into just eighty pages in the original, has a dual narrative. Each page is divided into two: the 'super-text' in the top half of the page narrates autobiographical stories of the protagonist's subaltern world, while in the lower half of each page we find a string of three discursive monologues by three old Dalit characters. Through the lively, irreverent prattles of these three characters in the 'under-text', Kali constructs commentaries on the psychology of terror and counter-terror, the state machinery and Indian federal edifices, and the Dalit's experiences in colonial and post-colonial India.

These nineteen 'fictional' and 'nonfictional' narratives, with shared themes, contexts and locales, revolve around the poor, the sick, the aged, the abused, the oppressed and the silenced, voices from the margins that are in sharp contrast to the larger-than-life characters of the *Shanti Parva* of *Mahabharata*.

Shanti Parav is thus truly a post-modern novel that is discursive, polyphonic, and even absurd. Kali's genius lies in his inventive, stylised structure which subverts traditional, linear fictional narrative and challenges the reader to acquire new ways of reading and interpreting a text. Through this master stroke in *Shanti Parav*, Kali has opened up new possibilities in narration and narrative technique.

Capturing the spirit and feel of the narrative in English is in itself a difficult task because of its structural and stylistic dynamics. With due diligence and erudition, Neeti Singh—an established academic, writer and poet herself who moves comfortably between Punjabi, her mother tongue, and English—has not only translated but rather transcreated Kali's text. I personally think that translating, *Shanti Parav* is a humongous and extremely challenging task, which Neeti has delivered exceptionally well. I have genuine expectations that readers of English will read *Shanti Parav* with the same keenness and interest that it has been hitherto read with by Punjabi readers.

Manmohan

Note

*'Dalit writings are victims of state's intellectual mafia: Des Raj Kali', *The Tribune*, 20 June 2016, Jalandhar.

Translator's note

Born Punjabi Sikh in Gujarat, to parents who had migrated from West Punjab during the 1947 Partition, I have my roots in Punjabi on the one hand, and on the other is my acquired taste for English language and literature through long years of convent schooling and a string of university degrees in English literature. Both moorings have stood by me in my intimate Punjabi readings of *Shanti Parav* as I have struggled, sitting in Gujarat, to comprehend and translate the language and ethnography of indigenous Dalit Punjab, conspiring in the process, to cajole, stretch and refashion in English the bohemian and somewhat rowdy dynamic of the Punjabi threshold, to find English parallels ('objective correlatives', as Eliot would put it) through which to transplant and hybridise in translation this robust, rustic language and world upon a new soil—so far removed and foreign to the sense and sensibilities of the original.

As a translator and an academic, and as a dissenting soul that writes poetry in English, I have thoroughly enjoyed translating Des Raj Kali's novel and have often employed my right to artistic license in the process of translation-as-transcreation. The aspiration was to translate not just the language but also to bring alive in English the vigour of the Punjabi, to retain and recreate the energy and emotion of the source text, which is the unbridled fruit of a matrix of significations—what Itamar Even-Zohar terms as 'polysystems'—that make language a genetic and truly a lived experience.

The proletarian, Dalit context of *Shanti Parav*, for instance, is harsh and pedestrian, and the idiom that pervades the novel is therefore robust, full-bodied and shockingly unpretentious.

It is an idiom richly embroiled in the sweat and sorrow of the Dalit psyche with its trajectory of survivals mapped by poverty, addictions, subversive gendering and counter-aesthetics.

My task as translator was further challenged by the deep chasm that separates the two languages and the people who habitually speak and think in them. On the one hand was the semiotic of the ostracised Dalit—our *desi* version of the 'Homo-sacer'—and on the other was the class of the privileged English-speaking potential reader. Translating the coarse narrative of the hapless Punjabi Dalit into English—which operates from a space of relative privilege: intellectual, cultural and social—proved to be a creative and intellectual challenge, indeed.

Translation in a way pre-empts a meeting, a merger of the source and the target text, and this fact of translation—the merging of two disparate polysystems: the Punjabi of the marginalised Dalit with English, a language of the empowered—raised several linguistic and semiotic challenges as one tried to yoke together paradoxical worlds in fabricated, extended metaphors. One had to struggle between retaining the robustness of the original and fish sometimes for English parallels and alternate 'objective correlatives'. Take, for example, the case of the foul-mouthed fat woman in 'Kavi o vaach' (The poet speaks) who showers upon her father the choicest of expletives, and has the whole street shell-shocked. While translating the young woman's anger and the local cuss words into English, I chose to rework the original syntax and sentences in such a way as to reproduce the energy and emotion of the Punjabi Dalit Doabi* dialect. I settled for a mix of English and some common Hindi-Punjabi words like *sala* and *moora*, but in such a way so as to convey, if not the exact meaning, at least a sense of the original idiom.

In 'Ikk sharaabi shaam' (A drunken evening), there is this poor drunken rickshaw puller who has temporarily adopted a house that is being constructed in the neighbourhood for sleeping in at night. The poor fellow, who habitually sings film songs and babbles to himself each night, raises quite an alarm in the neighbourhood, until he is nabbed one day and is discovered to be a harmless wretch. In the original Doabi dialect, the prose is musical as is also the Bollywood song, which, however, falls flat in its English avatar. After weighing the options, I opted to retain the original lyrics and also provide the English translation as mellifluously as was possible. The rhythm and structure of the English sentence, too, I have experimented with immensely; the effort has often made me stretch the limits of accepted English idiom, and it is here in the borders between two languages that creative syntax happens and new English writing surfaces.

Let me acknowledge here that my tryst with practical translation and the skills of the craft have come to me solely from my experience of translating Punjabi (and a bit of Gujarati) poetry. I began way back in the early 1990s with select Gujarati poems of pre-Independence poets for a poetry column for *The Indian Express*, and then went on to translate the Punjabi verse of Guru Nanak for my PhD in Bhakti in the year 2000. Bhai Jaita's epic *Sri Gur Katha* came up in 2013, and recently I have been working on translating into English a hundred selected poems of Peero—the first woman poet of Punjab. Des Raj Kali's *Shanti Parav* is my first attempt at working with Punjabi prose. As a student it has brought me much enrichment and growth. Insights into practical translation that are shared herein have emerged solely from my personal experience of translation. They have been documented solely from a desire to add my two bit pence drop in the ever-expanding ocean of translation studies and hermeneutics.

In the interest of both the writer's and the reader's comfort, I have taken the liberty of retaining in translation certain typical Punjabi words which I have then explained by inserting a sentence of my own in the flow of the main text. There are no footnotes but some terms or concepts that need explaining are listed in the glossary.

Also, in the nonfictional part of the novel, which consists of three long monologues by three retired but dynamic Punjabi Dalit characters, there are subtle and graded differences in the language spoken by the three. PbhagMull Pagal, for instance, is a Doabi Dalit; he speaks the typical Doabi Dalit dialect. Professor

Jauhall is a Jat Sikh, and an intellectual who has his own academic drawl. And Comrade, who is a communist brahmin, speaks with the passion and gusto characteristic of a Leftist! The longwinded and often loosely constructed sentences of Comrade and Pagal were challenging in terms of interpretation—especially as they dealt with little-known facts of state politics and ideology in post-Partition Punjab. I have tried to retain the original length, syntactical flow and energy of Kali's sentences to the optimum extent possible, but have modulated them wherever required. To reproduce the world of Kali's *Shanti Parav* in English with utmost sincerity to the original and with as much equivalence in terms of resonance, synergy and intellectual strategy, and yet to fuse into the narrative a sense of élan and English chic—that has been my effort. I hope that it has paid off. The subtle nuanced differences in the babbling monologues of Comrade, Professor and Pagal can get lost in translation, which is a pity. An attempt has been made, nevertheless, to offer some sort of a nuanced version in this English translation.

I have tried to honour the interests of the writer and also kept in mind the facility and comfort/discomfort of the target audience. To the achievement of this end I have resorted to all possible tricks in my arsenal. It would be fair, therefore, to describe this text of *Shanti Parav* as a translation, transcreation and a rewriting of the original in English.

The experience of translating Des Raj Kali's *Shanti Parav* has brought me thrilling adventure and growth. It bewildered and challenged me initially as it is supremely experimental, and I had never read anything like it before. Later as I researched, read, reread and studied the text in depth, it opened up a chasm of interdisciplinary interactions, explorations and subversions pertaining to history, literature (literary form, narrative and theory), subaltern and cultural studies, anthropology, ethics and politics. Here is a text that qualifies as Roland Barthes's 'readerly text'; here is Mikhail Bakhtin's novel as 'discourse' that is 'carnivelesque' and 'polyphonic'; here is a book that deconstructs at multiple levels. Jacques Derrida would have adored it! Here is a path-breaking work in Dalit fiction that Babasaheb Ambedkar would have been proud of, and which I humbly urge Georgio Agamben to read.

Vadodara **Neeti Singh**
4 November 2019

Note

Doab, literally, two waters, is the region between the two rivers Sutlej and Beas. Doabi is the language spoken in that region.

About the novel

In this novel of mine I have taken a format from the *Mahabharata*. That format is of *Shanti Parav*—the twelfth book or *parav*, post-battle, in the *Mahabharata*, it makes an aesthetic presentation of actions performed in the past, and thereby attempts to rationalise and justify them. On the one hand is the aggrieved Yudhishtir; on the other hand is the warp and weft of it all. In addition to what was done, and is now past, are the deliberations of the sages of the soil which it tries to instil in the collective conscious of its people—this is an aspect which is significant and deserves serious reflection. This twelfth parav of the *Mahabharata* is of extreme importance as even today, we can see recurrent manifestations of its line of thought—it is an ideology that has continuously reproduced itself. It is a means of entering the folds of our *raj tantar*. It is a pathway to an understanding of the theology of our *Hakkam Pirs*—our so-called sages patronised by the State. Noteworthy is the fact that this entire ideology was conceived and sculpted in the aftermath of war, when there was peace. These are deliberations produced during a period of peace. It is noteworthy to see how State violence is condoned and justified as righteous, penalty, too, is justified, the State is hailed as ideal, and the sages lauded. There is plenty here that needs to be scrutinised with diligence.

However, in the novel, the mode of 'time' alone has been deliberated upon. Just as *Shanti Parva* of the *Mahabharata* is located in the post-war period, my novel, too, has been conceptualised six decades post-Independence. Just as *Shanti Parva* has been scripted with the intention of justifying the past and sustaining hegemonic dominion, my novel, too, is written with the intent of investigating the past, searching for the underlying roots, and thereby forging a future that offers a new map and vision.

Shanti Parva is the discourse of the rulers, the *Hakkam Pir*. My novel, however, is the 'angst of humankind'. It endeavours to raise the concerns of people at large. I have tried herein to understand the anguish of their hearts and have tried to gauge the role of the State amidst it all. I have also tried to map the *tantar* or the structure of the State. Yes, the method adopted herein is that of 'time', so that a rethink may be facilitated. For that very reason there are in this text some elders who interrogate or perform an *atam manthan*, which amounts to a rigorous churning of the soul-conscious. Since the basis of their prattle is politics and political thought, I have utilised the conversational mode. It is possible this may irk some scholars; however, I wish to present my point of view with clarity. This is my *rajniti*—my strategy, and my politics. It must therefore come through with clarity. The characters are merely an excuse.

There may be misgivings with regard to the format of this novel as well. However, I did that which I felt was right. Several political allusions and names were there, which I have changed ever so slightly, and scripted. There were those who helped me and supported me throughout this enterprise; they include Dr Seva Singh, Dr Sarabjeet Singh, Dr Sukhdev Singh, Lahori Ram Baali, Tara Mal Paagal, Comrade Manohar Lal and Geet Chaturvedi. Sukhvant Artist, by drawing from the blueprint of my brain, has blown life into the title. Obligation to all of them is on my head.

Towards Amrit Grewal, there is immense gratitude in my heart, for all the intricacies of political governance and political economy that I learnt from him in the initial days—all that learning has stood by me in the writing of this novel. He is the champion of my grasp and insight into political economy.

This novel of mine occupies the second place in a series of *nar nataks*.*

> *Naadanda: Kshatriyo bhaati, na dando bhootim-kshanoote.*
> *Naadandasya prajaa rajya: sukhme-dhanti Bharata.*
> The circumvention of *danda*, penalty, befits not a kshatriya. It neither brings eminence to the Raja's stature nor permits the

monarch that desists to partake in the joyous consumption of the fruits of the earth. Also deprived are the denizens of that Raja who turns his back upon the duties of *danda*. In the land of Bharat, their share in the spoils is withheld, too.

Avinaashosya Satvasya nipto-yadi Bharat.
Bhitvaa shariram bhootanaam na hinsaa, pratipat-spate.
O Bharat! If it is ascertained that the *jiva*, the soul is immortal, then no act of extermination can possibly violate any life form.

Athaapi ch sahot-pati: sachvasya pralaya stathaa.
Nashte sharire nashtam spaadu-vrathaa-va spaatita-yayabham:
And if to patterns of physical birth and death we ascribe the conception and cessation of the *jiva* soul, then in that case all the tenets of the Vedas must stand cancelled.

—*Shanti Parva*†

Des Raj Kali

Notes

*A *nar natak* literally means 'the world theatre' or 'theatre of men'.

†All of the above *shlokas* on *danda* and *satta* or power were uttered by Draupadi, wife to five brothers—the five Pandava princes in the *Mahabharata*. Those were times when the matriarchal system prevailed. The *Shanti Parva* or the Book of Peace is the twelfth, and the longest, of the eighteen books of the epic; it has three sub-sections and 366 chapters. The English translations of the shlokas from *Shanti Parva* here, and at the end of the novel, are by Neeti Singh.

Consider this

No character or event of this novel is imaginary. Manmohan Singh here is our very own Prime Minister Manmohan Singh, and PbhagMull Pagal is that same old Dalit leader. If any character of this novel reflects you or your life, then it is not a co-incidence; it certainly is you. Begin reading the novel from the top half sections. During this reading, you will be guided on the reading of the lower half.

Daybreak

In every house there lives a *buddhi rooh,* the spirit of a hag. Her hoary white tresses dishevelled. Gleaming in the lines of her face red eyes shot with threads. Split ears, earrings dangling at the edges. Her lacklustre visage wilted sometimes and sometimes fresh as morning dew. Not the spirit, but the body, the hag's body perhaps dwells in here. Like a toy with a winding key it goes on and on blathering, 'tarr-tarr...'. What you speak neither you know nor the one who is listening. Yes, gradually in the listener's mind, the cacophony begins to collect and fester. 'These people

Comrade's prattle

Look here, the state or other powers that be, they all take the support of terror. It may be any form of government, meaning even if it is the current democratic raj, state that is, be it the Indian democracy or the Amrican democracy. The state and sections of the state's allies—both those that are privileged and those that are not privileged by the presence of the state—they always employ power to counter their opponents and each other's opponents. Their strategies of annihilation, which are crude methods, are known as terrorism. Unless there is dialogue...but even then there are strategies of suppression...if cannot manage anything. What will they do? We the damned and old, of what use are we now? We do not even remember. Even basic bread is denied us. If we go to other people's homes they feel embarrassed. What will others say—that we lack even the crumbs of shame? Winter! Days of cold, you'll catch a cold... *Bawasir* has troubled me no end. I'm now ripe with despair. That isabgol powder, I don't know where I kept it. Since last night I can't find it. Now if the stomach clears, then alone will the bawasir go. Once the bawasir dissipates, it will bring some relief to the haemorrhoids. Who will explain all this to them.'

The listener's blood rises in a boil all across the body and clambers up to the brain. 'Phoon-phoon...'. Through the nasal tract such sounds emerge and emit. Thoughts in the brain like green peas in boiling water dance a jig. Like girls that are stupid and disorderly, or say, like a bull that is enraged. No, in fact like an enraged, poisonous cobra. 'Phoon-phoon!' All sorts of sounds

lawful means are employed for dialogue, then it is a different matter...but if crude methods of coercion are employed, that is terrorism. Terrorism means stopping people from verbalising their concerns and aggressively imposing upon them one's own perspective or interest.

This terror is not just an issue of today. It is the term that has become popular of late. This *terror—I mean there was also the terror of Changez Khan who used to charge at us; that, too, was terror. Then there was the terror of feudalism as well. The era of slavery that was, that, too, was terror. There was the terror of the Roman Empire, of the slaves who led lives of bondage and labour—that, too, was a form of terror. And the terrorism that is saffron, we shall talk about that, too. Another thing about terrorism is that it festers among the minority community; it is not of the majority. The minority that believes it is unable to get support for its perspective, that is how they think or they have* begin to sputter. Then the face and head will get wrapped in the *rajai*. Tarr-tarr, like a hammer it will continue to ring in the ears. Tarr-tarr, the ayurvedic roots of *guggal, luban* and *mushakpoor* will char and release fumes. She would then have begun to take the *tuhni*—fumigation. That is why I say she cannot be a *rooh*, a spirit. It certainly is a body. In spite of the fact that the fumigation drives us, the rest of the family, berserk, she is least concerned. She only concentrates on the treatment of her bawasir.

Nothing seeps through her brain. Her brain it seems has congealed. Her rooh, too, is congealed rock. Soul she does not have at all. Though from time to time the rooh does peer through her eyes. Sometimes it peers from the face, too. One does not suspect without reason. There is a body. That too of rock. Poker-faced. No, the bugger is a *manoor*—an ill-baked brick, defective and discarded. With spiked edges. It neither grows nor swells. Perchance if someone were to run into it, they would be torn asunder.

in them a rage that their vision has weight, that they have to get their perspective across to the other side, to the non-believers. Then they resort to coercion. Since they are fiercely passionate about the issue, when they use coercion they resort to violence as well. They beat and kill and explode bombs. Because they think that the people have to be terrorised so that they do not stand with the protector, that is, with the state. So they become far-sighted and annihilate the state and erase state authority. So that people may lose faith that the state cannot protect them.

...Now as it happened in Punjab, the police that was there, it would do nothing. The 'exective' that was there was crouched in fear; they themselves would take gunmen as escorts. The deputy commissioner used to walk out with ten–fifteen sepoys. The judges that were there in the small courts, they would not pass any judgement. They would simply change the structure of justice, change the modus operandi, and in effect cause the

The reek from the fumigator has crept up the nostrils. Strange odour, this. What kind of bloody remedy is this? Fumigating the constipated piles! She props herself very comfortably, cross-legged, upon that iron chair whose seat, like the potty box chair for kids, has been cut round at the centre. Bloody hell, what must the craftsman have possibly been thinking when he made it! At the time of illness this very chair was used by her for defecating. Now that she has begun to move around, it is being used to fumigate her piles and her haemorrhoids. Eventually she developed an attachment for the chair. She would keep cleaning and scrubbing it. Place it in the sun. Share her woes and wellbeing with it. 'You alone are my support in this old age. Otherwise there is no one left that will care for me. May God not give such old age to any human. May He summon them all to Him!' But at night if a dog howls, more than the dog, it is she that does not allow us to sleep.

suppression of justice. Meaning, to counter terrorism, the state would employ strategies of counter-terrorism, and that is the point from where state terrorism kicks in. Because otherwise the cycle of violence never ends. The lawful means that are, I mean the existing laws that there are in a democracy, they are all routed through acts of evidence. Who will give evidence that a bullet was fired? From where did the gun come? To prove all this becomes difficult. Then as a rebuttal to terrorism comes state terrorism. This *is what all states engage in. It happened in Europe, too: the Home Act. The Home Rule they established, the rules that Birtannia formulated...now that Brazillian that was in Amrica...the police got wind that the man was a terrorist and they chased after him...he came out and they shot him without even interrogating him...! And not one, they fired so many bullets!*

'Mother-f****r Amrica!...Mother-f****r Amrica!'

I, too, am held ransom by god knows what kind of illness. Without a peg at night, sleep just will not assail me. At daybreak I spring awake. In the shadow of alcohol when does a man sleep? One merely slips into stupor. When perchance, slumber does begin to seep, the old crone decides to clamber up above me. How many times have I resolved to install an English commode in the latrine downstairs—it would end the daily pother. But what to do, the required amount of money is never at hand. The house expense itself grates a very salad out of me. Also, there are times when the money spent on liquor smarts... Sleep just will not descend, what is one supposed to do?

Bloody money problem is dogshit. It spares nobody. Each one of us gets trapped in its clasp. Close relatives forget to remember us. Forget to mix and mingle. Don't know what the mindset transforms into. Now consider my own father. Till date he refers to himself as godfather—*saeen*, a title used by a sage or a *sant*. He

...Did you say something? To me? No? I thought you did! ...As I was saying, that is terror. This could also have been its motive, not that the killing was done purposely; it could also have been done just to frighten the people. The state, that is, does not have an upfront, overt agenda. It has a twisted agenda—to spread terror among the people, kill one or two just like that and then say that they were terrorists. The Amrican state was so petrified that it failed to distinguish between good and bad, terrorist and non-terrorist. For someone's convenience that Brazillian was tagged a terrorist. They fell upon him and sieved him with bullets. I mean, they could also have fired just one bullet in his leg and wounded him. But no, they straightaway killed him.

The term terrorism, that is, is a recent coinage. For us, too, this Pakistan... Now the thing is that before the war of 1971, there was a war in 1965. Because the establishment of Pakistan was based on the conflict within Bharat, on the enmity of the Hindus.

talks of *darveshs* and Sufi mystics. Harps on the essence of life and says, 'If you find it, be grateful; if not, then hang on to fortitude. Ride each moment on the back of gratitude. If intense rage assails you, shrink its size from large to miniscule'. However, whenever he spoke to me, he would drop the middle of the sentence. A live wire tremor runs through and singes my heart. Let not this addiction to money puff you with pride, brother. Matters of money are sheer dogshit.

The Congress—that is, the enmity of the majority rule—was born from it. The English instigated the Musalmans, they got Pakistan made. Wherever the English went—Philistines that they were!—they divided! Korea they divided. In Vietnam, too, they brought a divide. This was their colonial power. This was their character. Now...

'Black Angrez mother-f****s...Black Angrez mother-f****s!'

Who is this!...look here now, do not use cuss words. The matter at hand needs careful examination. Understand the manipulative character of the colonial rulers. When the colonisers were threatened, consider who were the people they sucked up to and which were the alliances they forged. First and foremost they roped in the Awadhis—I shall tell you their story as well. Then they inducted the Mahars from Maharashtra—the Mahar regiment was the first to be established. The Marathis were

One evening

Who knows why all the women of the *mohalla* have fallen ill. Eyes sunken. Faces stark ashen—yellow! Feel scared of them. Hair all dishevelled. Even the clothes they wear these days are strange. Obese! That's what they all are getting to be. Their bodies are getting misshapen. From one end of this street to the other, these shack-like homes climbing tall and gaunt in their ramshackle ruin, they look so, so very obscene. Umpteen times have I desired to caution her, listen one ought not to sit on the

not taken in, though. Later the Mahar regiment was dispersed. Now, post-Independence, once again the Mahar regiment was launched. Meaning, the colonial rulers specifically enlisted those segments that were unhappy with the colonial raj. Now the raj that was in Uttar Pradesh comprised Musalmans; they felt they had been dealt a raw deal. The brahmins from Awadh and the Rajputs considered themselves a united force. They established tulkedars, *revenue department officials. Land was given to the Musalmans during the time of the Nawabs. It was like this: there was no system of pension to compensate all those who had served the state; they used to simply allocate some land to them in the form of grants.*

...and the feudal rule that was in existence. In Hindustan that is... Consider how the reign of Babur might have sustained here in Hindustan. Babur arrived. Babur won a throne in Hindustan. He consulted Beram Khan, and reached Delhi after

threshold during the hour of vespers. It is ominous. Brings bad luck. Bloody like someone who had come asking for loan, and were waiting. Never sit on the threshold. Many a times I have felt that I should talk to my wifey and send across a message that the reason behind her adversity is this same habit of sitting holed up on the threshold during the hour of prayers. Then this one begins with her half-dead, flaccid eyes to gawk intently at all that come and go. And the other one, even though she is quite well, consequently begins to feel kind of ill, unwell... Does she have a husband or not? Even this we are unable to gauge. But she does apply lipstick and put *sindoor* in her hair-parting. She wears clean clothes but they are terribly creased. Come evening, she dresses her hair, too. Children play in the street. She does not even glance at them. Just seems sort of lost. Damn the sick woman!

Now the cleaning women of our lane, most of them come from the mohalla behind. Slowly and steadily they, too, have

defeating Panipat. He said we have a strong army of twelve–thirteen thousand. But the army is exhausted. A new battalion cannot be brought in at this point. Since Babur was an Uzbek, a large portion of his troops were either Uzbek or they were Pathans. The Pathans hailed from Kabul, so their loyalties were two-pronged. Babur feared that the Pathans could switch their loyalties at any point. What should be done? Along with Beram Khan and three–four other advisors—Ibrahim Lodi was also among them—a discussion was held, and it was decided that the darbar *be summoned and a formal declaration be made that the status quo would remain intact. Meaning, whichever tulkedar,* jagirdar *or whichever revenue officials that were there, whoever was already established in the existing system, all that was expected of them was that they acknowledge Babur's dominion and supremacy. Babur's dominion was accepted, and so were* become obese and are losing shape. Those of them that are lean, their eyes have acquired a frightening, stark whiteness. Many of them have even stopped talking. This Krishna who used to come to our house, she has erupted all over with the ringworm. Now her daughter comes to work. The girl has got her ears pierced in devil knows how many places! The very sight of them is enough to terrify a person. Or you could say one is invaded by nausea. She wears jeans and her arms are swathed in glass bangles. On her nose she wears a ring. She is not twelve yet. But her eyes, too, have acquired the same pallor. You cannot look her in the eye. They give you such a fright. A strange terror seems to seize the mind. The cleaning woman at the neighbour's has also been bloating up. The flab falls flaccidly around her stomach. That on the sides of her dorsum, too, has begun to sag. The face is heavy—it has begun to resemble a frog's. Damn! Darkness on all four sides! Compared to other women, however, all these ones

the other conditions that were proposed. Those who refused to accept them were compelled by means of force. The Rajputs of Rajasthan had refused to accept Babur's dominion; they were prevailed upon to do so by use of force. Such is the structure of the state. The state itself resorts to accessing the support of terror. To some extent, the state even exerts it.

Now those that indulge in lathi-charge, they also adopt crude methods. Lathi-charge is also prevalent in Europe, but it has declined there somewhat now. Here in India, however, it is more common. Perhaps because people here are coarse. There not as much. Now in Amrica, too, fifty lakh people had gathered. The state declared that after eight in the morning, entry would be denied. People began to pour in at night itself. By eight o'clock in the morning, twenty–twenty-five lakh people had gathered. There were women there as well, but no one harassed them.

here wear cone-tipped bras. This is the sole and singular feature of attraction among them... This, however, is an amazing thing! Well, even the infections they catch are of the weirdest sort. Sometimes they support their continuously bloating stomachs with their hands and walk.

At a snail's pace they move, dragging their feet heavily as they move. From this very drag the rising sound of 'skrruch-skrruch' grates harshly upon my ears. I detest women who drag their feet while walking. My wife's paternal grandma also lives with us. She is in the habit of dragging her feet when she walks. I rise early at dawn, so I know. From the kitchen to the room in which she sleeps, she walks about fifty times. It is due to her 'skrruch-skrruch' walk that I am unable to sleep. Troubles me no end, this sound. Then they also have multiple problems with their uteruses. That's why the slow drag of a walk, like ailing snails. Sometimes they walk with their legs akimbo. *Yaar*, being a

Nothing went wrong. It was peaceful. But just because our people are not yet fully aware of the various strategies of statehood, our state oppresses them, through coercive ploys!

'Kale Angrez mother-f****s!...Kale Angrez mother-f****s!'

Someone seems to be shouting expletives! Who knows who it is! Anyway, I was saying that the terrorism that has prevailed in Hindustan, it is very essential to understand Pakistan's role behind it. When the 1948 war happened, they tried to snitch Kashmir. This strategy of theirs had come to them from the Angrez; it was not some brainchild of the Pakistanis. The possession of Gilgit town that was they had taken earlier from the ruling king himself, during the Second World War. Because the borders of Gilgit that are, they touch Afghanistan. The borders of Gilgit also touch the borders of Chinese-occupied Turkistan and several other borders, and these they had taken on lease. There was one English captain Galib who formed a squad of Border woman is so, so, painful. Nowadays many of them simply opt for a hysterectomy. There is no other cure for it. Otherwise you can't even move around. The weight is bothersome. Now if a person can't even walk normally, how absurd is that!

My maternal aunt's daughter-in-law has developed knots—rheumatoid nodules. There is inflammation in all her joints. Even her face is inflamed. This time again she is afflicted, and pregnant again! Bloody, what is this! On the one hand she is so ill, and then to subject her to the mumbo-jumbo of voodoo! What is her fault if a son was not born, eh? They have three daughters, and all healthy. Now what was the need for more? Besides, they have also adopted the younger brother's son. What more do they need after this? But their mindset no one can fathom. Who could ascertain uncle's thinking? It was *Masar*'s boorish, tent-like idiom that I used to fear, and that kept me from ever paying him a visit. As if he ever cared to enquire after my wellbeing and bliss. On my

Scouts there. Before 1947, when the English had surrendered Gilgit, there was also one Brigadier Ghansara Ram; he was made the governor and sent to Jammu by the Raja *of Jammu. The Border Scouts, they killed him, and the Gurkha sipoys there were, them, too, they killed, and declared themselves free. All this happened with the connivance of the English. Yes, they did not succeed in their motive, but the enmity with Pakistan was established. Then the war of 1965 broke out. In that war, for the first time, they dropped their men at Aadampur, and in Kashmir. But the local people did not give them shelter. So they got arrested in Kashmir as well as here. This was confirmed during the war of 1971. It was established that if Pakistan were to do anything in Hindustan, they could not defeat us in an open war. They must prepare an army which fights under cover, with their support. For that purpose they began to groom terrorists. Some were inducted from Kashmir itself. Some they brought from outside. Some were incited in the name of Islam.*

arrival he would remark, 'Now you are settled in the city, eh? ...so how are your mothers-in-law? They live with you right? Hmm.... now you are all grown up. ...and besides, who are we to you!' And more...I don't know what all he used to blurt out. It would exasperate me. *Masi,* my aunt, would endeavour to restrain him. Masi, one's mother's sister, is like ma, hence ma-*si*. But he, tight-fisted son of the father that he is, he used to blow his own trumpet. Well, now that he is no more, why badmouth him behind his back. But he went just like that. Poof! Riding piggyback upon the intoxicating potion of *bhang*. He was consumed by Sorrow. His body had become pulp. Sorrow gobbles a man up like blood. From without, one cannot tell what's happening. Within, however, the person continues to hollow out gradually, bit by bit. Masar went through the same trajectory. I received a phone call. I had just reached the hospital when, outside at the entrance itself, I ran into my cousin, my maternal uncle's son.

Then, in Punjab, the manner in which the Akalis declared that the Sikhs were marginalised, so also the Punjab state... this thought had spread like an angry stain in the hearts of the people of Punjab. Despite the fact that a lot of the preliminary development work post-Independence was done in Punjab. The greatest investment that was, was incurred in the Bhakhra Dam project. When the Bhakhra was built, at that time Hindustan used to produce two lakh metric tonnes of cement. Seventy thousand tonnes of cement were consumed in Bhakhra per month. So, of the total cement production of Hindustan, forty to fifty per cent was consumed in the Bhakhra alone! The Bhakhra is all cement. And the steel rods that were used, Tata Steel used to manufacture those. The steel rods made in Mandi Gobindgarh used to be so small-small! The larger ones were made by the Tatas. All that steel used to come here to the Bhakhra—to get such a colossal structure standing on its two feet! Then the canals were built and

'*Pbaaji*, our *Phupharji* is no more.'

'What!'

Phupharji was my fraternal uncle. After that I had seen his dead body. Just didn't get around to talking to anybody. My laptop was slung on my shoulder. I had expected to leave for office directly from there, after seeing him. But who could have imagined...

...Anyway, it is good. We got to know later that they would be handing over the body the next day. Masar's son was yet to arrive from Dubai. I don't know why, but somehow it felt good. Right, so...then we would take up this matter tomorrow at the time of cremation. Now I couldn't suddenly land up like this in office, not after I had informed them about Masar. It somehow didn't feel right.

much else was built...all because the Akalis kept on instigating, provoking.

But in truth, the Akalis did not have any justifiable slogan. Power, too, would keep slipping from their clutches. The reason was that in Haryana, which was vast, the Hindus were in majority; therefore, power would always evade the clasp of the Akalis. Eventually, they shrank the size of Punjab. Earlier they used to say that the Sikhs are marginalised. Later, after the Punjabi Suba was established, they claimed it is Punjab that was being marginalised. Just as earlier power had been with Majhe, it now passed on to Malwe, and Majhe got neglected. There was a lot of poverty on this side...in Gurdaspur and other areas. And joblessness and frustration. No development ever happened here. The generation that had been a young lot, even among them the pile of debts rose high. Another line of thinking that then gathered momentum was that things, in order to be acquired,

The poet speaks

In the capacity of an author I'm going to disturb you just a wee bit. Actually, with reference to the context, characters, and ambient mood of the novel, I feel that you need to be furnished with certain details which, in a way, will facilitate your reading of it. You will then be able to dig into the deep soul-space, the *antar-atma* of the characters, and the route will be found thuswise. This is also because the characters in this novel have an extremely dense stream of consciousness; if that goes askew,

must be grabbed by force, and the smugglers that were from Pakistan, meaning the nexus of smugglers that was, the older ones of the lot began to spread terror; they first became atank-vadi, *then they graduated to being smugglers. Those smugglers used to smuggle* narcote*—narcotics. Along with narcotics, the guns began to arrive. Also some other things.*

Then Bhindranwala arrived on the scene. He was brought in by the Congress, which then began to use him. Around the same time, Subeg Singh, also known as Shabeg Singh, joined Bhindranwala. Now Subeg Singh of the Indian army was a hero of the 1971 Bangladesh liberation war with Pakistan. He was the one who had trained the Mukti Bahini...the youth force. And so he was decorated with medals and feted for his role in India's victory in the war. Now in the army, the punishment that is perhaps the severest of all is that of cashiering. Subeg Singh was stripped of all his medals and his titles; he was dishonoured then rest assured that you, too, shall go off course. But if you are equipped with some knowhow of the site of action, if some clues or landmarks are embedded in your mindscape, then it will be more convenient. You might spot such lost souls lurking in familiar, haunted alleyways or glimpse them in the middle of a crowd, going their separate ways. Somewhere or the other, with someone or the other, you will be able to relate to them.

Now, as for the source of the seeds of this novel, I shall delve into that right here. I found employment in a Hindu daily which had newly opened office in Punjab. The office was located at one end of Jalandhar city. We commenced our duties. It so happened that I was unable to bring along my afternoon meals. Around two, however, hunger pangs would assail me and I would step out, scouting for street food in kiosks and food carts which, however, failed to lure me. Then on the Lado-wali road (now you must keep this in mind, Lado-wali is a character who will appear later in this

and disbanded from the army. What happened was that some jealous sepoys abetted him to lead them in a fake rebellion and then conspired to have him thrown out of the army. Subeg Singh, whose heart was brewing with rage and humiliation, then joined the Akalis. When the state was trounced and the Akalis began to hijack the state, once again the state stood in their way. Then it became difficult to save the state without resorting to terrorism... and so there was state terrorism.

> 'Mother-f****s Angrez! Black-faced!
> Mother-f****s Angrez! Black-faced!'

Then came the army. And then came Gill. Then Gill and Beant Singh forged a partnership. Beant Singh had not been able to win elections as an independent candidate, but he was now pushed towards a win. Before him the Akali—Barnala—had been pushed to victory. Barnala's win was also a conspiracy; the Congress had weakened. But that conspiracy did not work. Then K. P. S. Gill novel in a very strong and *shaktishali* manner), from a railway track I spotted another food cart. To my heart's eyes, it seemed like one perfect world. Beautifully arranged, spotlessly clean vessels. Sparkling clean. The water pitcher covered. Every object, every item tidily placed. The hygiene complete and impeccable. The plates neither laced with grease nor with the impress of water. This world pleased me utterly, and I merged myself with it. In this world were some aspects of immortal grace—all the things that were kept propped on the food cart, and the bread-maker herself, a tall woman of tanned complexion whose big-big eyes could have slain anyone. Her husband merely engaged himself with serving the *rottis* and making tea. Or else he would collect stray abandoned glasses scattered all over the place. Two tiny little daughters whose features resembled their mother's and a son who, after school, would head straight to the food cart. The existence of the rest of this world was caught up in the process of

and Beant Singh were brought in.... This state terrorism and anti-state terrorism, you see, are just like siblings, like brothers; there is very little difference between them. The state resorts to terrorism for its own purposes just as the others have their own axes to grind. So look here, in order to spread corruption and terror and mayhem in Punjab, the state released its own men. Some among them were even made black commandoes. Even rapes were perpetrated through them. Meaning, they spread corruption, degeneracy, violence and fear in the name of the terrorists so that the people would turn against them. When that stage was reached, the terrorists began to be arrested in large numbers. People's hearts were soaked with hatred and fear. The state choreographed the performance of its acts in such a way that it prompted the people to turn against the atank-vadis.

'Black-faced Angrez mother-f****s!
Black-faced Angrez mother-f****s!'

comings and goings. The rickshaw-*walas*, the impoverished poor, the beggars and I.

In this way, about a year and a half sped by. This world, the odour of their sweat, the details of their visages had gotten etched in my heart and mind. Those large eyes would often erupt even in my dreams. A fragrance would arise from its colours. Her daughters attended to every need of mine with special care. How diligently the son would pour water—not a drop dared spill here or there. However, what happened is that one day their food cart vanished from the site. The track was vacant. A world had suddenly disappeared. Had the earth swallowed it or had the skies consumed it? I was upset. I went back. Unable to concentrate in office, I retraced my steps to the site once again. Not a bird or soul in sight. Not a soul used to be seen anywhere before, so who could possibly be around now. I had never noticed any specific regular customers; all had appeared as beings in transit,

...Now I will talk about Pakistan. This is essential in order to understand terrorism. Now earlier the Pakistani sarkar was very much a feudal sarkar. The Muslim League had no clout with the Pakistani government. In Sindh there was the Congress sarkar. Muhammad Sayed was a nationalist. Among the bureaucrats, some were Iranis. The Nawab of Awadh was one. The Nizam of Hyderabad was from the family of Noorjahan. And the others there were all Musalmans; they all migrated to Pakistan. The Musalmans who live here in Punjab are natives of the land, the mulk. *Very few families stayed back. The rest all migrated to Pakistan. They reached Karachi and settled down there. There in Pakistan, the state structure as it was, its power dynamics and control was all, in a way, army-centric. The army's control subsumed the landowning jagirdars as well. That is why it has not been possible to establish civilian governance there. Democracy just cannot be sustained there in Pakistan. Whenever they find themselves unable to achieve a targeted end, they just bring in*

coming, going, coming, going. So there was nothing, no scrap of information that I could lay my hands on. I kept thinking and thinking. My heart continued to leak out on patience. Then the next day, too, a vacant track. On the third day, too, a vacant track. Then suddenly I asked a news reporter, who responded very casually that, 'Their son was kidnapped. Three days have passed, he has not been found yet. The poor lack clout even with the courts and police. Sobbing and shrieking, God knows where they have gone off to!...from which state they hailed even this nobody knows nor anything about their local residence here...!'

My heart gave a sudden lurch and went still.

(Now dear reader, from here if you read 'Retired Professor Jauhall's prattle', the novel can be comprehended even better.)

We can now discuss the novel's context and settings. This is a crowded area of the city of Jalandhar. In a nook along the main

the army. There was this Bhutto before; now it is a Zardari. There are big jagirdars, feudal lords we can call them. Lakhs they own, two-two lakh acres of land each. Feudalism will just not end. It will not end for the simple reason that the Musalmans were landowners first.

Here in Punjab, too, we should have had the jagirdari system which prevailed at the time of the Mughals. Agra and what was then the Punjab region was under the state. It had once been under the raja's *dominion, that is, the land belonged to the Mughal* badshah. *The farmers used to pay* lagaan *directly to the badshah. The feudalism that prevailed there was off the limits of Lucknow. Here there were no mighty feudal lords. Even now, if a land record of the region on that side is required, they must go to Agra to get it. In Punjab, there was no mighty jagirdari system to reckon with as such. It was prevalent only in the Province of East Punjab States' Union (PEPSU), 1964.*

street which is perpetually jammed, a tiny lane threads in. The lane bends in quite close to the Gurdwara Sahib. The next bend is to the right hand of the doctor's clinic—that same doctor who has for a long time now been doling out medicines in a benevolent way. Earlier for a prescription he used to take fifty paise; then he began to charge a rupee, then two rupees, then he moved to five rupees and nowadays he takes ten rupees. His visage has remained quite consistent, the same as it was ten years earlier. His hairs, too, have stayed intact, untouched by the appearance of salt. I keep pondering how he must have passed so many women of this locality under his thigh. His visage itself is tell-tale. The people of this dense locality lay such faith on him, too. Actually, when a woman shares her ailments with the doctor, she partakes of all liberties at that very point. Then or thereafter, for the doctor, it is time for hay-making!

Amritsar, Jalandhar, Ludhiana did not have any jagirdars; they were directly under the king's dominion where peasantry of the middle scale prevailed. The peasantry in Pakistan was entirely under the feudal jagirdari system—particularly in Sindh and off the limits of Multan. Afghanistan and Baluchistan, however, were regions of the tribals. That region is not at all agrarian. In all of Sindh there prevailed the jagirdari system. Those who were agricultural farm hands or kheti-war mujare*, they were called* haari*. There were those who did the sowing, whom the landowning farmer could employ and expel at any point in time at his own whim. Theirs was a life like that of slaves. And for the Musalmans who had gone from here, the absconding Hindus had abandoned so much land behind that for each Musalman who reached there they had launched a scheme of one* kila *of land per family member. Meaning, if somebody had a five-member family, then five kila of land was given. A kila was a measure*

Anyway! This very lane is that primary site of action. The neighbouring *kasbas* and suburbs of Jalandhar are also included in this. You will observe here a significant influence of Kapurthala. The impact of Kapurthala is immense here. Relationships are an amazing thing, too. The character whose stream of consciousness we will now examine lives in a house located right across the ruined palace—that is, in a quarter of the *mahal* that has still survived. A very grand building it is. It is said that this palace has been constructed along the lines of French architecture. It was the residence of the brother of the Maharaja of Kapurthala, after whose name this mohalla acquires its name. Due to the English, rather it was Queen Victoria's decision, it was decreed—as a fallout of the case they had filed demanding that Jagjeet Singh relinquish his claim over the reign of the provincial state—that the brothers of the Maharaja of Kapurthala reside outside the city limits. Besides, by then the British were quite overwhelmed by the tide that had

of 4,840 square yards of land, approximately an acre. However large a number they were, and regardless of their caste, each person was given a kila. Even if they were a family of Marasis. *The Marasis were low-caste Musalman bards who used to take horses to ceremonial wedding processions. Even the landless folks received it. But later on the kila per person scheme went bust. Not all of them were farmers, you see, so they were unable to cultivate the land. They had no farm implements either. Then the jagirdars purchased those lands, and they purchased them cheap.*

'Pakistan is a mother-f****r!...Pakistan is a mother-f****r...!'

Then Pakistan commenced with its indirect war on this side. It first began with Kashmir. This was an indirect attack. All the ammunition for it used to come from there. Help used to come from there. It all boiled down to the fact that they thought swept across the nation, the tide of the Congress. Special care was therefore being taken to maintain the provincial states. In lieu of this a decision was taken in favour of Maharaja Jagjeet Singh and his two half-brothers—born of the womb of Chhotti Ma—it was decreed to put them on a share of allowance money. Simultaneously it was also decreed that they shift residence to some place outside the jurisdiction of the province of Kapurthala. Thereafter they came to Jalandhar and settled in this very mahal.

Now this mahal has a very strange story. It's a long story. These days a widow occupies it. Afflicted with leukoderma, she has turned white as a sheet. When and if she colours her hair black, she turns into quite an apparition. The skin around her eyes has escaped the impact of leukoderma. Therefore the skin around the eyes retains its original colour. If it weren't for the leukoderma, her skin would have been lustrous and fragrant. Leukoderma has played havoc with her features, almost obliterated them. In

Hindustan was invincible, that they could not weaken Hindustan. Do you know that once Laldenga had written a letter to the separatist leader Mann? Laldenga was the leader of the Mizo National Front; it was he who had led the rebellion in Mizoram. When once again the Mizoram pact was signed, Mizoram made peace with Laldenga. They disbanded the chief minister and invited them to form their own government, meaning people were demoralised when they said to them that you make and run the state machinery, run the state. But in his letter to Mann, Laldenga wrote:

> *'I rebelled for seventeen years. Those who used to provide me with help, monetary help, arms and ammunition, when I said to them at the time that I declare independence, give me recognition, they had refused and said that we shall not give you recognition. I realised then that they use us—to weaken Hindustan. They are unwilling to give us political rights. So then I asked them, why get people killed? Why*

the foregrounding shine of the leukoderma, they appear flat like wooden boards, truly—like standing sheets of water! She works in some bank. About her comings and goings only this much is known that sometimes she hangs her laundry on the terrace of the palace. Sometimes she comes up to scatter millet for the sparrows. On holiday mornings, after bath, she spreads out her hair and sits in the sun. Or else we see her when she drives off to work in the mornings on her scooty. The main door to their house opens on the other side from my protagonist's home and is closer to the other side of the street. From their terrace, these people can clearly see hers for they are right across, but not her entrance door. Who all might be coming and going, at what hour she might be leaving, for which place, they cannot tell. Along with the widow dwells her *dadi-sas*, that is, her grandmother-in-law. My protagonist has never seen her. But he has often heard the robust tenor of that extremely frail-bodied hag who goes 'tarr-tarr'. You, too, will get a taste of it.

> *get young boys killed? So I suggest that you do this: Ask the powers that help us to grant recognition to Khalistan. They will refuse.'*

That is the reason why Mann cooled off—he cooled off after receipt of this letter from Laldenga. Mann was in jail then. Laldenga had sent him the letter in jail. Those people will never give you recognition. They will make you fight, get you killed. Get the boys killed. You, too, will die. But they will not give you recognition. They will shut you up in prisons. And nothing will come of it. Because the state of Hindustan is so very strong; it can battle for ten–twenty years, it can get two lakh men killed. There are so many who can enrol as soldiers. And your fight is with the state—do not mistake it for the Congress sarkar. This is a fight with the state. Understand the difference between the state and the Congress. The state is a merciless thing. Then all the Khalistani separatist leaders realised that they must withdraw, and it was

A count of all the houses in and around the street totals to just six. That is, if the palace is set aside. The house behind the palace which faces my protagonist's house is amazing as well. At first there were three of them: the mother, son and father. Father an electrical mechanic, mother a retired teacher, son an MR or medical representative. When the protagonist moved in here from the village, a fat and healthy girl used to frequent the house. She is the daughter that got into a love marriage with a boy from Jalandhar. Then she delivered a baby boy. The boy, too, came to live with them, and began to grow up there. The retired mother's head turned grey in a matter of months. Then in about a year's time that girl emerged once again. She had gone off to study some course of sorts. Somewhere far. If she came in-between sometimes, then nobody knew about it. But when she returned a year later, the entire street got to know of it. What is scandalous is that she spit cuss words at her father like the

imminent that they do so. The Rajiv-Longowal compromise had arisen from this same line of thought. Then they brought Beant Singh and Gill to the forefront, and within a year's time they had beaten a retreat and sorted out things.

'State is a mother f****r!...State is a mother f****r!'

Now I shall tell you about the terror of the Naxalites. They said kill all the landlords, take their land and redistribute it among the landless. They said the people will join in with you. But no, the people got terrorised. I will tell you something. There used to be the Communist Party. When B. T. Randive became a communist leader, many of his comrades were in prison at the time. They said you shout slogans in the jails. They said the people are all with you. The people will break the prisons and get you released. They said the people are all against Bharat sarkar. They will sacrifice their freedom for you. But exactly the opposite happened. The comrades who were in the prisons were beaten men folk: 'Sister f****r! PIMP!...You bastard! Sala!...Have some shame. You lived all your life as a *MOORA*! Coward!...You DOG! Pimp! Have shame!' And not once but every third day her kinetic scooter would come sputtering down the street and from the first floor of their house, like a meteor shower the cuss words would begin to ensue. There is no one who can question them. No one dares to. People say that the person she berates as a coward is himself a monster who erupts like a typhoon if anyone dares even speak to him and digs his talons into their cheeks... But when his daughter yells at him, he dares not utter so much as a squeak. This shrewish, Chandi-like aspect of the girl was witnessed by people of the street one day before her wedding as well.

Anyway, the house adjacent to their house is no less! The wife is a ravishing beauty, while the husband is a commonplace shopkeeper with the face of a hamlyn monkey, a very *bijjoo*! Runs a small shop in the nook of this same locality. A hand-to-mouth

and butchered to death. No one outside protested. Not even ten men. Meaning, that when you wrongly assess your strength and begin an agitation, it acquires some shades of terrorism. It seeps into every party each time that a faulty assessment of one's own strength is made and the strength of the state is underestimated. Party must understand that the sarkar is of the Congress... They forget the power of the state; they forget what the state can do.

The state as it stands today, the monopolists and the industrialists who are in it, they do not consciously wish for violence, do they? They do not even aspire for the suba-states *in fact. They introduced the VAT with the intention of levying a single tax. They introduced many other such taxes, as a consequence of which the strength of the subas got considerably depleted. It has all gone to the private and the corporate sector. Earlier, visitors used to parrot the names of Tata, Birla. Does anyone now even remember Tata and Birla? All the sarkars,* income, and two young daughters. They were only recently married off. One of them had a love marriage while the other's was arranged. Both are short. But in this locality, one thing is amazing—in every house some girl, boy or the other has got married for love. As such they are carpenters by caste. Their boy is married into a khatri family while the daughter is married into a family of goldsmiths. Across is the house of *Chaaih*. People from the Jhang Sayal region of Punjab address their mothers and grandmothers as chaaih. All of her three daughters have had love marriages. She had one boy; he, too, fell prey to a love marriage. Chaaih has gone to him these days. He, however, is the most amazing character of this street. The tiniest of thefts or alliances of the street are chronicled in the silt in Chaaih's fingernails. Now if she were here, she would have investigated the matter and the reasons that had driven the girl to shower such bitter abuse upon her father.

even the Leftist sarkars now extend invitations that please come, bring us capital investments. Those who once used to mock in the name of Tata and Birla...that same Comrade Bhattacharya now says, come Tata Sahib, put up a factory at our place. We will give you land free of cost and loan, and no taxation in the first five years. We won't charge you income tax either, you come to us. Does anyone take names now? Nowadays those who were once considered class enemies are no longer class enemies. They are all invited guests now. And they all strut around with so much pride. Earlier it used to happen that when they asked the prime minister for time, they were not given any. Now it is the prime minister who asks them for time. He goes to Ambani in an airplane and says, Ambani Sahib, give us some time. Mittal Sahib, give us some time.

'Nizam is a mother-f****r!....Nizam is a mother-f****r...!'

The house of the protagonist is three-storeyed. Two rooms on the ground floor are rented. Mother and son are the landlords. The son is of a marriageable age. They are brahmins. Sometimes the elder son returns home drunk, leans against the door and keeps blabbering. In stealth from the younger son, the mother siphons off some money to him. Due to these antics of the elder son, his first woman left him. The second one that he seduced into wedlock was from the Chihuran community. The Chihuran are folks who would carry water for the village people, cook for them and render other such services. She was the offspring of a prostitute, a *randi.* Lived in a *kutcha* mud house of barely ten square feet. In that very same house the elder son joined her after marriage. Doesn't do a thing for a living. The mother-daughter duo have organised a food cart in Malka Chowk. All day long they make rottis. The rickshaw-walas are all their customers. Many a time this fellow is seen sitting there, staring away, muthar-muthar,

However, it is not that the state does not change. The state also changes. Now in Amrica it has changed, hasn't it? There was such a boil among its people that they ensured it changed. The state did change. The President of Amrica could have asked them to stop drawing their salaries, reduced their pay or put a curb on them. You spend five-five lakhs per man and you sit in ships and come. Then you ask us for money from the state and ten-ten lakhs you spend on your parties. Then in the evening you celebrate. Fifty thousand you spend on a massage. Could Bush have said this in earlier times? And under the pressure of its people the state does not swell with arrogance either! Now all the King-kungs and the dictators who used to be puffed up with pride and power have metamorphosed.

Now there is yet another side to terrorism, and that is where it joins hands with religion. And that is when it becomes even more deadly, the way it has in Pakistan. There is terrorism in Europe as well. It's happening in Italy and elsewhere as well. But

like an owl. Then in the evening, after some wrangling, he snatches from them some liquor money. He also has a small daughter.

Right under, in the room below lives the old hag, the Buddhi, tarr-tarr. The bathroom as well as the toilet she uses—the one with the English seat—is on the first floor. Her residence, however, is below. A temple has been installed in her room itself. On the upper floor lives the protagonist's family: three people and the two themselves. Upstairs there are two rooms. There is a kitchen, a bathroom and a storeroom. The steps climb up to a third floor. Both third-floor rooms, which are in the custody of the protagonist, have been converted into a library.

Well, this location and the details of the characters you must keep in your mind. There is much more that is attached to them, therefore I have endeavoured to take you out of the novel and tell you so much, or you could say that I have pointed out to you the actual route to entering the novel.

those forms are not attached to religion. They desire a different set of targets. But where religious frenzy enters, there it becomes fatal. The religious fervour, the junoon *that is, has prevailed in Punjab. When religion fuses with terror, it becomes a potent threat. This, which terrorises people, is many a times abetted by the state as well...it has happened so many times in Punjab that the state did not perform its* dharma. *That is state terrorism. Now in Punjab the violence that happened during panchayat elections, that itself was an aspect of state terrorism. When this increases slowly-slowly, then matters reach the gun. This is terrorism. Meaning, ever since the state was born, terrorism was born and it has been going on ever since...*

> 'Mother-f****s, all of them!
> Mother-f****s, all of them!'

O yaar, where has this mad fellow been brought in from? Why? God knows who all he will curse and abuse!

A nightmare

I fail to fathom why the heart continues to moulder in a dread-grip. A strange confusion pervades. Anybody may pass any random remark, and my heart, I do not know why, goes absolutely still and is suffused with cold fright. I do not know what happens. Tension thickens. Blood pressure rises. The head splits with pain. Sleep vanishes for just no reason. Now I can't even answer back the one that has passed the remark. But the dread elicited continues to spread. Can't figure out a thing. Then, when matters

PbhagMull Pagal's prattle

We are village dwellers from Pharala. Earlier Pharala was in Jalandhar district itself; Nava Shaher was the tehsil. There used to be two to three tehsils or revenue units in one district. Now that Nava Shaher has become a district, village Pharala has gone into Nava Shaher. It is a little distance from Sanwa. In Pharala, our ancestors used to live. The mainstay of our elders or the mainstay of the entire schedooled caste tribe's elders was not agriculture. There was a reason for it. That reason was the Intakaal Araaji Act which had been formulated in 1900, and according to which we did not have the right to purchase land.

come to a head, I begin to feel that the task was a mere figment of imagination—nothing at all. Due to this very mindset, the issue of land purchase was delayed. Delayed? I had wished in fact that it would run aground and fail. The brothers were to purchase land. It is their money that was to be spent. To me they only said this much, 'Come along, come with us to the court'. Well, the very act of going to the judiciary had begun to feel like venom. The matter reached such a point that the broker who was selling the land in the 'red line' scheme discovered that his land actually fell in the ambit of the revenue department and had been allotted the *khasra* number. Why then should we get the deal registered in the 'red line'? Wah! Anyhow and any which way...the work was stopped! The brothers accepted my suggestion.

I breathed a sigh of relief. Not exactly a sigh of relief—my sense of dis-ease had in fact stretched further. Brother was saying that he would convince them to register in accordance with the

Any land. Even if it was one marlaa *of land, we had to buy it in someone else's name. And the land would remain in that person's name alone. We would just continue to live on that land. But if that person resorted to any treachery, we were undone. After the emergence of Pakistan, by the blessed intervention of Dr Ambedkar, the Intakaal Araaji Act was dismantled. At last we received the right to purchase land and become house-owners. Now the houses had to be built on land. They couldn't very well be built in the skies, could they? And if the land itself wasn't ours, where on earth were they to be built? Besides, we were slum-dwellers living in rickety, ramshackle shanties. We would bake the bricks ourselves. The rich, who had the permission to buy land and build houses, they used to take all the good, strong bricks, leaving behind only the* manoor, *bricks that were over-baked or defective. We would build our homes by layering these* khasra number. I wondered when again would we be required to make a trip to the *tehsil* office. After visiting the courts my mind was in a strange spin. A restlessness assailed me. I had left quite early. Hadn't even bathed; thought I'd wrap up the task and bathe on returning. Thanks to the mild *talkhee* sun of early March. I went and stood in front of the court canteen. Many advocates were just arriving, crisply attired, wearing ties, or ties that were pre-attached. Very disciplined. But their visages bore the impress of crooks. Bloody inflictors of penalties. Thieves of some site. Never must one trust them. Look here, their trade is incredible as well.

Then the court clerk arrived. He, too, wore the same harsh expression as the advocates. Close upon his heels came two boys who were typists. They spread their table and then ambled off across to play cricket. How incredible was this. One way or another, they managed to convert life into a play. Thereafter

manoor and plastering them with gara, *a brick-red dye made of mud. Therefore, ours were homes that could be called deficient or defective or manoor!* Manoor-*homes!*

Lying in a ramshackle kothri *of sorts, PbhagMull Pagal's eyes begin to gleam. He attempts to look outside. His gaze runs into the wall across, returns and burrows itself in his* gadholi, *the patchwork quilt covering him. He clears his throat and spits the phlegm into a kerchief. One feels disgusted. The Professor who has come to meet him has run thin on patience. Restless, he looks here and he looks there. Now, in the dark recesses of the kothri a soft light has gradually settled. In front of it hangs an old photograph. It is the young PbhagMull. Holding a pen in his hand, in a posture of deep reflection. Extremely charming. It is a painting. His own nephew has made it. An amazing artist he is, but the liquor has consumed him. He now paints and sells posters for a paltry ten-ten rupees in the hope of buying cheap country liquor.*

arrived many gloomy long faces. A prostitute also came. This was the one who lived at the tehsil office itself. On arriving, she bent low in the doorway and she touched her brow to the threshold. This, my friend, is the means to her sustenance. I salute her style and bearing.

Well, whatever we had come here for was accomplished. Then on the third or fourth day, brother got the land registered under the 'red line'. On seeing the recommendation the tehsil officer, who had earlier resisted, accepted twelve thousand rupees, and the registry was done in brother's name. Brother's phone came, and a cold tremor ran through my being. But I agreed, said I would come for a very short while just to take a look at the land papers. When I reached the court, they had already got the deal registered. We returned home together from the court. Liquor-shiquor was consumed. My head was fuzzy with inebriation when father sneered and flung a taunt at me, 'Why then, now

PbhagMull's breath seems to be even now and constant. He addresses the Professor. 'Our elders have set off, friend. Now let us undertake some work. The status at work was like this: those who were sweepers were happy to work but did not insist on being paid in cash for it. They would expect in return only some food in the afternoon. The chamar's *job was to make footwear and supply them as and when required; in exchange they would take home a fixed quantity of grain every six months.*

> Money is not to be taken. We are not sellers. Only grains will be acceptable.

They were those who worked in the village. All these mansions of the Sikhs were built in whichever raj that they were built. But the ones that were built in the raj of the Sikhs were all made by us. Because we used to bake bricks as well. Many chamars used to bake bricks in those days. As for garbage, the chuhras *or human scavengers used to collect it. They would collect the bricks along* the papers are okay, *na*?' I did not respond. But inwardly, tears of blood began to swirl. So that brother may not get wind of it, I gulped down my peg quickly and hastened home. On returning, I found that the keeper of my house, the *gharwali*, being tired, had fallen asleep. I did not wake her up. I quietly picked up my *rajai* and tiptoed to the library. All night long father's acerbic words burned my ears and I continued to grieve. Bugger! Flung me out of the house, and still he wears the garb of goodness! He never did sympathise with my compulsions. Always spun tales about me.

God knows what all he has said to outsiders. My father has himself maligned me, saying, 'He lies at the drop of a hat.' Father cannot see me happy. I, too, despise him immensely. Am I not your offspring? You spent so much money on the elder ones, taking loan upon loan for them. When it was my turn, what happened then? Did a snake cross your path? And besides, now

with the cow dung refuse and give them to us. In the cow dung refuse we would bake what are called chhotti intt *or small bricks. We also baked bricks that are known as* Nanakshahi. *We used to do all this work. And what did we receive in exchange? Only* rotti *to eat. We would take our women along. They would run the* chakki *and grind the grain for the horses, and there were songs composed by them:*

For your horses I grind grains
O Raja Ranjit Singha

'So she kept grinding the grain. She, too, would eat only rotti. No wages were given to her either. It is once again by the grace of Babasaheb Ambedkar that the Intakaal Araaji Act was ratified. And that we became owners of land and houses, and began to receive money in return for our labour in the form of daily wages. Otherwise, no one else has been able to procure any money for us as wages.'

you also have with you a capital sum. Did I not work with you? But no, what it is in his heart I'm unable to gauge.

I kept on weeping all night long, in convulsive sobs. In the morning my wife came in apprehensively and asked, 'Darling, are you upset with me?' I thought, why trouble her? I said, 'No, no. It's just that I thought you must be exhausted. I ought not to trouble you. But I have been grieving all night.' She pressed me close to her bosom. 'Why? Just yesterday you received such good news!' 'Yes, perhaps that is the reason I wept, being unable to tolerate such immense happiness.' Why I keep her in the dark about these matters even I do not understand. Then it suddenly slipped out of my mouth, 'But dear, last night I stood outside for quite a long time. Neither your aunt would wake, nor Buddhi, our old hag. Then Buddhi got up and opened the latch, and she glared at me as if I were some common ordinary lout... That is why I did not waken you.' Wife became very sad. She began to kiss me, and

The Professor needs information regarding just this. He is neither interested in listening to PbhagMull's ramblings nor does he have any sympathy for him. He just wants to get his work done. For work on the Dalits, funds can be procured from any quarter, and it is easy work, too. PbhagMull has already gauged this, though he has not yet traced the root cause behind the Professor's sadness and self-pity. Before the Professor can say a word, he continues, '...All right, so this was the general context so far. Now I shall tell you my own side of the story.

'So there was no source of earning for our father and the elders then. That part of Pakistan had just been newly established. Since it was newly established, the schedooled castes that were there in the village had taken up jobs as labourers and servants in the farms. Government jobs were available, too. But government salary in those days was thirteen rupees. Whether one worked in a municipal office or elsewhere, even in the military, it was just

said, 'No my love, you shouldn't have done that. You should have woken me up. If you had lain next to me, I would have awakened automatically. Yesterday I was very exhausted. Besides, I had also been fasting all day. Then this tarr-tarr of yours, too, had eaten my head off. God knows what all she nattered away. Her piles have ripened now. Wherefrom will she get any rest. But she does not listen to anybody. Goes on blathering...goes on blathering...'

This tarr-tarr, I don't know from where she came into our house. I just cannot comprehend a thing. Lice will not leave my daughter's scalp. In the process we even got her head tonsured. Rubbed all kinds of ointments from all over the world. But no, the lice will just not relent. For a day or two the head becomes clean, and the third day again they seethe, kulbul-kulbul. The same way I'm unable to figure out from where this tarr-tarr landed in our house. She is the reason that my home does not feel like home to me. I feel as though I am living here on someone's charity, that

thirteen rupees, you see. No other posts were available. There was one Musalman fellow from our village who was a doctor in an animal hospital. He said to our father that here you are living an idle life; either you take a dumroo *in hand and go about asking for alms in the name of Gugga Fakir, or you could howl loudly during the lunar eclipse and ask for alms in the name of a blind horse. Later you could even collect grain in the blind horse's name. Dumroo? Well it is a percussion instrument, hand held and shaped like a dumbbell. Then he said, "You come to me. I will give you thirteen rupees monthly. I'm a doctor there."*

Inspired by the offer, my father left for Shekhupura. The Shekhupura district headquarters was located between Layalpur and Lahore. My father got employment at the Shekhupura animal hospital and began to get a salary of thirteen rupees. As for the rest of us, our mother and the elders of the family made someone is giving me alms and I am a beggar. Am unable to build a roof over my children's head. That I cannot give them rotti. 'If you could not serve them then why, why did you facilitate their birth?' I felt as if the Buddhi tarr-tarr had climbed over me. I had no home; my father had thrown me out at the onset. Now I shan't go there ever. This home, too, does not belong to me. No. I belong nowhere. I have no place.

'My love, what is it that blights you? Why is your heart so weighed down with grief? Please tell me. Did Buddhi say something to you in the night?'

'No not at all. It's just that my heart is heavy today. Don't know why. You don't worry. Go make some tea for me.'

'First repair and cool your heart. Stay quiet! Then you'll get tea. Else you'll get something else...'

My heart burst into joy. The gharwali went to make tea. My thoughts began to leapfrog once again. Last night's dream began

dung cakes. As it was an animal hospital, they would make cakes of animal dung. And the potters would come and take them away—in those days dung cakes were used for burning in the potters' kilns. Today a dung cake sells for half paisa.

'...Oh dear! So perchance we had strayed into the Pakistani side. And there my father took up a job. At that time the British government had done one good thing, to which the Arya Samaj had also contributed: they had forged a rule that we Dalits be given admission in government schools. But we used to carry jute gunny sacks from home to spread and sit on the floor; we were not allowed to sit with the other children. We would carry our slates and bags as well. So my parents put me in a school in Shekhupura. It is a fact, and partly fate perhaps, that I passed primary school, and then the matter came to high school. In those days high school was under the charge of George Pancham, *that*

to stir in the mind. That I've gone to the village. Drinks are doing the rounds along with friends. I'm sharing with them childhood memories of being the brightest student in my class. I'm narrating to them how I had rattled off the multiplication table of 175 before the teacher. Hearing me speak, my father used to say, 'Ninety per cent of what he utters is false, which you may erase...'

The dream that followed this one I cannot recall. There was a lot of anger in me towards father.

is, King George V of England. I got admission in high school, too. But we could neither study Punjabi nor Hindi; we were taught English. Studies in those days were far more elaborate.

Anyway, so I was then studying in class eighth. When I was studying in eighth, at that time the Hindus held a conference in Amritsar. The Hindus held a conference because those that were philosophers among them had realised that the country would soon be divided. In spite of Jinnah's crusades, the Musalmans wanted that these people should stay with them, so that they could claim a larger land share. They, too, had established societies. For this very reason they organised a conference to which they invited Dr Ambedkar. There is one Amritsar Sikh Missionary College. In this missionary college the Sikhs also held a conference—surely that was hypocritical. What was the motive behind it? The reason was that we Dalits were very close to the Sikhs. They used to work as peasants. The chamars and

The philosophy of beggars

What is the need here for fear? Why should I fear? Have I eaten something taken from a pimp of a *kanjar*? What is it that compels us to get enmeshed in the trappings of relationships? Why should I needlessly hang their problems around my neck? Besides, at the time of marriage they never mentioned any such thing. It was divulged much much later. Such were their ways. Well, never mind. Since the matter was such, I agreed. But all that transpired earlier in utter confidentiality should also be recalled

the chuhras also worked in the fields alongside the Sikhs, head to head and shoulder to shoulder, drawing furrows upon furrows in the soil. Whether it was the kilns that needed to be built or the grains that were to be roasted, anything that needed to be done, joining head to head, we would shape the mud bunds for their fields and furrow beds. In their homes we would work as farm hands for which we were given a handful of grain. There was a nearness, a proximity that we shared with the Sikhs. But with the Musalman traders and the baniyas*, there was none at all. This is a fact. In that conference, I mean in the conference of Sikhs in the Sikh Missionary College on his very first visit to Amritsar, Dr Ambedkar Sahib, too, had agreed. At that time there used to be an English doctor amongst us who was of communist leaning. He would tell us, "Look, your leader has arrived! Your wellbeing lies with him alone. If only you would make the effort to go see him, to listen to him, you would come to know of certain things."*

now. Besides, her daughter-in-law had herself observed that just as Bhairavi took away her son, similarly now this one has taken him away. The gossip mill never ceases its spin, does it? Rather it sprouts blisters on its feet. At long last the gossip has spun its way to us. My wife says, they accuse me of taking away their boy; ask them if we ever ill-treated our family members the way their daughter-in-law has.

Now just consider the sort of circumstance she has put them through—it is blasphemous. She is in fact a Jat, and these are Chamars—bloody tanners! He is *Chachi*'s, that is, my aunt's grandson. Earlier they used to live in the Koona house. Then Chachi's son-in-law went off to Greece, and they really prospered. Then there is this boy Sindar. The one whom we were discussing is the elder one. He got educated and has now moved out of the village and gone on to settle in the urban estate of Jalandhar. However, brother is unable to let go of his attachment to the

Sir, we were just two or three boys. We were studying in the eighth, well built we were, we went to the Missionary College and stood at the gate. Now, Dr Ambedkar had to pass. O man let us at least see him! See what he looked like! So the first time I saw Dr Ambedkar was there, at the Sikh Missionary College. At the time Ambedkar Sahib, too, was very young. The lecture that Doctor Sahib delivered there, to a large extent, in terms of its philosophy, we did not understand at all. But we could sense from his words that this whole country was our enemy. From his talk we gauged this much that the entire nation was our enemy.'

The old hag prattling away with her tarr-tarr has muttered a lot many things to PbhagMull and left. He has now gotten into a frenzy. He has gotten derailed. The Professor is getting worried that his assignment might now be left half done. With great difficulty PbhagMull had come on the right track. Now who knows what might happen! Twice or thrice, the Professor has hukkah and to red nail paint. In the matters of their house, our Chachi has a huge say. This in fact is the root of all their troubles and conflicts. All her life, she did not allow anybody to settle down. She drives them all up the wall. She has tightened such a noose around the younger ones that gripped with disease, they lie here and there. Why not pursue the older family members, practice on them your conjuring and voodoo? Don't know what sort of a woman she is. I was very small when I used to see her stealthily smoke my mom's *hukki* which was usually kept covered; she would puff at it with such vengeance that any ordinary mortal would have died of the rough drag itself. Which battlefield is it that she aspires to conquer I simply fail to comprehend.

Now her daughter-in-law first took away their maternal grandson, saying that if you wish to get married to me then you will have to stay with me in Batala. Well, the reason he got trapped in this was simply that while chatting on the internet he

made attempts to draw PbhagMull's attention towards himself, but failed. Success at this point seems a difficult prospect. The old hag has spoilt the game that was being played so well. PbhagMull is gasping for breath. He has leaned back against the wall and is now sitting up. The Professor oscillates between hope and despair. Then after a few moments he looks at PbhagMull, and is amazed to see him completely relaxed and proceeding with his talk.

'The wave that the Ahmadiya leader from Mirza-Kadiya had triggered, that, too, was for this very reason. Following the Islamic rites of initiation, the younger, smaller lot of children amongst us used to walk across from under the belly of a trotting horse in the taziya *procession, surrounded by a sea of men flagellating themselves into a frenzy. Then they used to build small mud platforms and place five clay lamps upon them. In the homes of ordinary chuhras and chamars—whom we now*

committed to a relationship. Then those Jats turned out to be so incredible, they took the boy away with them. Six months the boy stayed there. Never mind. They agreed to him staying there with them. By and by the girl began to insist that he must not telephone his ma-papa. Then a curb was put on his meeting them. Then a curb even on his going out of the house. He was reduced to being a prisoner. The boy's folks began to get anxious. Threats to kill the boy, too, reached their ears. They were petrified. Then one day, the boy escaped. They snuck him here and there. The boy was in utter fright. Those people could have murdered him even. Then the girl's family along with the girl landed at their house. Mother and daughter entered the house; they ransacked it as they searched for him. 'Bring him out, you. You have hidden him. Speak! Where is he? Bring him out of hiding!' Meanwhile, we all kept standing in a state of sheer alarm. At the same time we kept saying, 'But he lives with you. He never even meets us.'

address as Valmikis—these customs were common. They would touch their foreheads to the ground in devotion right there. That is how it all was, and we experienced from this event that they, too, wished the same—that we be with them. In our community where we used to worship the brahmins, we also worshipped the Sufi pirs, the Pirzadas. *Sometimes we would worship a sacred herb. Then there was a pir's* mazaar *in the house of a landlord named Gulab. Gulab was older than Seth Kishandas, you see, so the mazaar was built in Gulab's house. He was not any pir-veer, but just like that. Following the wave which had begun in those days, we have been worshipping that pir, too. Meaning, that we continued to be Musalman also, and at the same time, to be Hindu also.*

'Dr Ambedkar thought or perhaps felt it was important, and so when the Partition was underway, he sent one person—this is a very long talk, it's a talk about history, so am cutting

Matters reached a climax, and that is when I came to fetch help. Said, keep some person at hand. Talk to some policewala. We are almost dying of this. Save the boy. You alone can save him now. Who knows what all they might do to him—he is a low-caste, *kumm-jaat*. If they come and set fire to our house, what will we do? You handle this. Come right away, we shall discuss this. Drop all your jobs and come this instant. Come and save the situation please. How could we imagine that we would have to use this ploy as well? We just said, even if they stay apart, let them. How were we to imagine that they had made a prisoner out of the boy!

Now many questions are passing through my mind. Why did nothing happen in the first six months? How come they arrived and did so much now? When we do not know the entire trajectory of the matter, how can we enter into a dialogue with them? Besides, we can be of use to them only if they had ever done us

it short-short—he sent one person from our community to the newly formed Pakistan Cabinet, that you go and represent the schedooled castes there. So even there a representation was made so as to take care of them. But that fellow could not settle down there. Later, he had come back by airplane. Doctor Sahib kept making efforts to strengthen the attempt. So our first introduction to him was at the Sikh Missionary College, but at that time the only knowledge we picked up from his lecture was that Hindus and Musalmans are both our enemies, and that of them, the Sikhs are closer to us.

'That is why when the Partition happened and when the massive movement commenced, there used to be one Master Tara Singh—here again I'm making it short-short, otherwise a very long talk it will be—Master Tara Singh was the president and Giani Kartar Singh was the secretary. Master Tara Singh, too, thought that Pakistan has become separate now, so in all

a good turn. My wife in fact is a fool. Says, never hold back in the hour of distress. I answered, in the village my father did not mention a thing; nobody summoned my brother either. Then why must I go? Why don't they confide in them? At the outset I refuse to get any work done for them separately. Besides, I'm already under a lot of stress. More burden I cannot bear. They have been telephoning repeatedly. I shan't take their calls either.

Outside in the street the Pingalwala's handcart has come. I turn and focus my attention on him. He is ringing the bell and asking for alms. 'Bhai, this is the Pingalwala's charity, it is a matter of faith, give brother, give whatever you deem fit. No loan is to be taken. May the Maharaj, the Lord incarnate Truth, enable you to give alms, O brother. May no one ever be compelled to give as penalty! May the Maharaj bless you, O brother. The lame and the limbless, all those who eat this will sing your praise, O brother! Tunn-tunn...tunn-tunn.'

likelihood we will have to stay with the Hindus now. If we have to stay with the Hindus then we should not spoil matters too much with them. First he said to them, keep the schedooled castes with you because they have been attached with you. This decision he had taken along with the representatives of the schedooled castes. It was discussed with Dr Ambedkar as well. There used to be one Seth Kishan Das; he, too, must have signed on the paper. Which means that we entered into a coalition with the Sikhs. Vaid Kartar Singh was with us. Master Sadhu Ram was also with us, who later became a minister. All of them were there together. Here in my house, too, a meeting was held. Due to that meeting they arrived at a compromise. The Akalis said we will give you these many seats. So our compromise was struck. We became workers. That, too, paid workers! Today I'm going to tell you something new. Charandas Nidharak continued to draw a salary. I also took a salary. There was one more Vaid who

Amazing, this fellow—on the one hand he appeals for alms, and on the other he fills the heart with horror. He repeatedly speaks of 'debt'. He speaks of 'punishment' again and again. At the same time he adds, may the Lord enable you to give in charity! Friend, these are incredible people, one cannot ever comprehend them. Look at the aplomb of beggars—the greatest of philosophers would begin to pale beside them! Incredible, my friend...!

was from Shimla who used to live here; he, too, was a staunch Ambedkari. His name has fallen off my mind now, but he, too, used to draw a salary. Here from the village, too, there were some fellows; all of us were paid workers. We used to receive money from the Shiromani Gurdwara Committee as well. In the gurdwaras, too, we used to go and lecture. In the process there was more closeness. When that closeness happened, the Congress got worried. The Congress said that things are going wrong, and that if all the schedooled castes go to the Sikhs, what will we be left with? Maulana Abul Kalam Azad was the Congress president in those days. Maulana Azad spoke to Master Tara Singh and said that if you enter into an understanding with us, we will offer you our support. They did arrive at an understanding. Akali Dal was broken and we became Congressi. These are things that happened after the formation of Pakistan. We then joined up with the Congress.

One drunken evening

Drank with Manni last night. It was awesome. Manni is my friend Sunny's brother. Incredible, isn't it. Actually, every human being is a boiling pot filled with god knows what sorts of stuff. The phoon-phoon sound is a constant backdrop. It is the same as the hiss that emanates from the tall clay pitchers that stand fermenting in the midst of sugarcane fields. The same as a serpent's hissing. The same as when that Buddhi tarr-tarr climbs up the terrace, and from my nostrils issues a snarling hiss.

'When we merged with the Congress, then the Congress said that well, these seats are yours, those seats are yours, and those ones are yours. Our deputation went. We asked them, which way shall we go? They said, Chhandda. *Get lost. We don't even regard you as a party. We don't regard you as a separate party; if you are with the Akalis, we can dole out a couple of seats in adjustment, they said. At that time there were seats, reserved seats, from the Mukeriyan constituency. I, too, got a seat. Well, I contested the seat because in those days the name PbhagMull had some clout. Even Seth Kishandas used to take my name because I had a strong voice. And I was also a poet. But we said that we do not want to take a seat. We do not want to take a seat because according to our calculations our seats must be separated. If you wish to give us any, then you must separate our seats, too. Maulana Azad sort of sidetracked the issue and said, never mind, we shall consider it. Then they took away some*

This sound seems familiar. I walk towards it. It is a matter of discretion; therefore I shan't spell out her name. Earlier she kept claiming that just for my sake she... But now I know better... Who doesn't crave bodily pleasure! Don't her actions convey it enough already! Anyway, what I was going to share is that the bathroom in her house is located at the rear of the house. Adjacent to it is the room of the neighbours who live at the back. From there to here and from here to there, sounds keep going back and forth. I brush my teeth. I harrumph. And am convinced in my mind that surely, someone on the other side is keenly keyed in to my manly harrumphing. In a lonely woman's home, a man harrumphs. Then he disappears. Right.

Here's another interesting incident that transpired yesterday. A colleague of mine, who is constructing a house in the Gobindgadh mohalla, was awakened in the middle of the night by a neighbour's phone call informing him that there is some man who visits his

of our members. After snatching away some of our fellows they gave a ticket to Jageer Singh Darad and to one Bhagat Singh; one was general sectary, one was vice president. Those two fellows they snatched away from us. They tore up our Scheduled Castes Federation. They gave them two tickets. After this the Congress decided to stir up some more initiatives. So when the riyasats *began to fall, they also gave a ticket to Sadhu Ram Sadar, who was from Phagwara. That Sadhu Ram went on to side with the Congress. There was one more person who used to live here near me; he was also given a Congress ticket from Rajasthan. So the Congress gave away three–four tickets. As a result of this, there was disunity. When disunity set in amongst us, Doctor Sahib said it was a bad thing to have happened.'*

The Professor has not asked PbhagMull a single question all this while. He fears that if he does, the session may again be disrupted. The old hag has made two or three rounds already.

partially constructed house every night and chatters away. He went running to the site. The house is incomplete. Even the doors have not been installed yet. In the room across is a drunkard, a poverty-stricken ragamuffin. They caught him by the scruff of his neck and brought him out. To avoid a hullaballoo in the street, we made him sit astride the motorcycle between us and drove him out to the open level ground. He was unable even to balance himself, sozzled as he was on half-a-bottle of liquor. First my colleague gave him two tight slaps and then inquired who he was. He was a Bihari from Bihar. Said, 'I run a rickshaw on rent and in the evening I return it. Earlier I used to sleep at the railway station. Then one day I came to this lane and found this deserted spot. Whatever I earn I spend it on buying rotti or *sharab*. I do not have a mobile phone. I do not talk to anyone except my own self. I talk to myself alone. Or else I'm fond of singing. I practise, do my *riyaz*!' And he began to sing loudly.

And every time she came in, the Professor's head would begin to reel. But the hag did not say a word. Yes, her eyes stayed riveted upon the Professor. He was unable to meet her gaze. He did not even understand why the old woman inquired if PbhagMull would get any money for this work or not.

'...am again talking in short-short. So Doctor Sahib made an announcement declaring the adoption of the Buddha dharma and said that all the schedooled castes should adopt Buddhism. Now, one massive fair used to be held near Phagware, in Chak-Hakim village. Very large numbers used to come to that fair. All of Punjab, people from all corners of Punjab, used to gather there. There was a Guru Ravidas temple nearby. The priest in-charge of that temple possessed a political sensibility and he had fought elections as well. Just like during the Baisakhi festival, an elaborate fair used to be held at Chak-Hakim as well. Indigenous desi footwear was made in Chak-Hakim from dohri khal *or*

Jahan kisee ko mukammal jahaan nahin milta
Kahin zameen toh kahin aasmaan nahin milta

A utopian world is beyond one's reach
If one gets the earth, another only the sky receives

Then he said he would stop coming here from that day onwards. However, my colleague intervened and said, 'Never mind. Until the house construction is underway, you may spend the night here, but do not make a ruckus and do not do your riyaz.'

Well, I was talking about Sunny and strayed off in another direction. Yaar, he is utterly, ruthlessly lonely, with no one to ease his existential despondence. Says today I was feeling sort of sad. The heart longed to take off to some unknown place. Sometimes the heart said I ought to listen to music. Sometimes the heart urged me to sit with someone and have a drink. When I suggested that these are symptoms that occur in the lap of desolation, Manni interjected, 'No, I was not sad at all. I don't know, it's a strange

double-layered hide to make it nice and tough. Those cobblers used to make footwear for us, too, and they continued to do so. But the breach had already set in. The divide had fallen upon us as well. When Doctor Sahib announced that we should all become Buddhists, those of us who had become MLAs, those of us who had progressed, those who had become leaders, they organised a separate conference in Chak-Hakim. They said, "If someone makes a fool of themselves, it is no matter. But no one should make a fool of the entire community." This was the issue that was raised. A poets' meet, a kavi darbar, *was also held to discuss this issue. I was a poet; so an invite was sent to me, too. I said I will not speak at the conference. That I was an Ambedkari and that I would continue to be one. You people decide what you have to do. Among them the first to give up the job was Lahori Ram Bali. Bali became a Boddhi. See, now that which is wrong must be protested—I did not become a Boddhi, but I opposed that separate* state I was in today. Anyway, when I telephoned you, you, too, were idle. So...this was fun. This is the first time I've sat with you. With friends we have sat many a times. There is between us also an age gap. Besides, it was always Sunny who used to sit with you; in those days I used to keep a distance.'

'Yes...! But where is Sunny these days?'

'He has gone off to Germany....He also did not shape up too well. I had my hopes for him, but he went off track. Pbaaji, you must have met my mother surely. Those who had wronged her, those who were her culprits, Sunny went down on his knees even before them. The same folks who live in the house across from ours...who own a depot. That is the house of my *Taya*, my father's elder brother. His wife, my *Tayi*, also happens to be my Masi, that is my mother's sister. In our house, Tayi was always at loggerheads with my mother and resented being questioned. Mummy had begun to keep poor health around the time. This

conference! Lahori Ram Bali was not called a Buddhist; he was called a buddhu—*a fool! This was a wave that swept away many of us. Many got caught in it, many were beaten up and many got soiled, too. There was much pondering and agonising over this camp and that camp. When such giant waves unleash, some get caught, some beaten, some in one way, some in another.'*

There is a glow on the Professor's visage. His purpose has been accomplished. PbhagMull, too, is in high spirits and continues. 'After that, maharaj, we began the Federation's work in right earnest. Some of the members whose names became popular thereafter had joined much later. Vaid Kartar also joined us later. So also Dr Bhagat Singh. Dr Bhagat Singh used to come and visit me often. We created a programme for him for he was a doctor also and he was into politics also. In politics you have no status. But your name can be established since you have a doctor's degree. Bhagat Singh was an MD. There are all mother-daughter duo would come every evening and besiege her with cuss words. Whip up a huge *tamasha* in the mohalla. Mummy, poor rag, would be utterly petrified. By and by her blood pressure began to rise. She began to stay unwell all the time. The very second day after she passed away, Tayi was to leave with her daughter for Germany. Her flight was scheduled for the next day. That evening, too, they had left her after a fierce fight. Mummy succumbed to a spasmodic attack of sorts. We brought her to the Palan hospital. I was much younger at that time, studying in class eight. In the hospital, mummy became dear to God due to heart failure. Tayi went and hid somewhere all night long, and her family members kept claiming that she was already on her way to Delhi—her flight was in the morning... I hate those people. They killed my mother. But my brother went down on his knees before those very people. Sunny had to go to Germany; so for their sake,

sorts of small doctors, but an MD is a big degree. We said to him, brother, you should go around the villages; you should attend to the chuhra-chamars and the disease-ridden people there. If you do not have the money then write them a prescription, instruct them regarding which medicine to take, guide them on how they must tend to their children, follow basic good health practices and other such things. Thus Dr Bhagat Singh's pictures, too, were printed in the newspapers, the ones in which he is examining patients. Along with him many more doctors joined us. Dr Narr, who was a staunch Ambedkari, also joined.

'...But ultimately to what end? No good came of all these things. The reason we did not benefit from it all was because the community at large, our own community, did not understand us. Today I have been lying in this cot for the last two years. Since two years I have been undergoing treatment. Not a single person from the community has ever offered me even ten rupees to go

he dealt me a tight slap—just because they would be hosting him in Germany.

'...They are aware of it. This is an incident of that day itself—the day when we had daddy's retirement party. You had all arrived. I and my friends had not yet arrived. We were all dancing. *Bhabhi*, my sister-in-law Kavita, she was also dancing with us. How happy we were! A song was playing: "the *chhotta dewar* is Bhabhi's *gehena*, he plays around in her proximity." We kept on dancing. But Hunni had poisoned Sunny's ears before bringing him to us. As soon as Sunny arrived, he stopped the music, forced the DJ shut. When I asked him why, without batting an eyelid he slapped me a tight one on my cheek. The problem was just this—why had I objected to Taya joining the dance party? They, on the other hand, had surrendered before Taya's family and gone down on their knees. Shame on them! In that very resentment he had dealt me a slap. That same day I decided not to live in that house

get myself treated. Albeit on Dr Ambedkar's birthday they do bestow honour upon me. The community has not evolved; it has not improved its understanding of things. We never used to draw any salary for our work. After the breaking of the 'compromise', we had responded in kind to the Shiromani Committee. They had then gone and joined hands with the Jan Sangh. Later, when there was a procession proclaiming the formation of a Maha Punjab, they began to talk about the formation of a Punjabi Suba, and turned against the Maha Jan Sangh. Such a huge procession it was! However, despite being in disagreement, they finally went and merged with the Jan Sangh. Till date they have remained merged with them. What I mean is that all this struggle of Dr Ambedkar's was from then onwards. Let me bring to your notice that the PEPSU sarkar fell. Once monarchy fell, the sarkar could be formed. Since sarkar had to be formed, the any longer. Now I live at my Didi's, my elder sister's place. I had insisted on renting an accommodation in some other locality, but *Jijaji*, Didi's husband, would not allow it and said you live with us only. Now, how easy is it to live in one's sister's house? I feel that now I must make my own house on top priority basis. Only after that will I marry!'

This one has got sozzled in a single peg itself. Or else there is a lot on his heart. The fellow's lost it in just one peg. Or again there is a heaviness in his heart. And I can't believe it—he is indeed an ardent fan of Lata Mangeshkar! Nobody is talking about that. Let me allow him space so he can sort himself out today. But he won't unwind so easily. Let me share my own stories with him. To induce him into confession I shall tickle him with my own. We are all selfish creatures here. Nobody is loyal to anybody, really. Not even one's father or mother. I'll tell you what all has transpired with me. A while ago we met with an accident, barely escaped

*Akalis approached us and urged us to favour them—*Tussi kirpa karo, *they had said.*

'There was one man of ours, Meeha Singh Gill, who succeeded in getting a ticket on the elephant symbol, that is, from the Bahujan Samaj Party. That party's agenda was to win Meeha Singh Gill's favour because their election was pitched on a single ticket. Bhai, if we get one seat on our side then we can form a sarkar, they said; otherwise the Congress will take over. Please make our sarkar, they said; that is they were suggesting that they could forge some sort of compromise with us. At the centre of all this was their candidate Gian Singh Rarewala. Also Bhupinder Singh Mann, the legal advisor from Patiala, who was at the centre of the Shiromani Committee. All of them came in their vehicles, made me sit in the middle and they took me along with them. We went to meet Doctor Sahib at his house. He was

death. We had telephoned home, too. You are aware that I live in the city. The village people had banished me. I was deeply saddened, and petrified, too. The chasm of death was long, long yet. Bruised and abandoned by death, I returned to the village thinking it would divert my mind. When I reached home, my father said, 'It is good you have come'. He should have told me that they were going in for the purchase of land, and warned me to carry with me some odd sum of money. But no. I was furious and burnt to the core. Bloody hell, till date nobody has ever asked me how I had escaped death. Not even for twenty-five paise had I ever depended on them... If you wish to buy land, go ahead; how is that supposed to affect me? From this very ire, I had blurted out that I had no money on me. I thought of how, like hell, I had barely escaped death, and these buggers were hassled over money! Rather than empathise or understand my perspective, father turned around and said, 'The place where you work, don't

sitting in the front, reading a newspaper. At that time they first asked me how I addressed the Doctor Sahib. I said that I touch his knees and greet him with "Jai Bheem". They said touch his knees if you like, if not then don't, it is your wish. They went and stood there, clasping and unclasping their hands. For five minutes they just kept standing there. Doctor Sahib did not look up from his newspaper. He just kept saying, "Hmm...Hmm" at intervals. As in, he would say, "Yes?" To which they would respond that they had simply come to see him. Then he said, "Okay, so you have seen me. Now leave, or talk, come to the point". Then they proposed that they would take Meeha Singh Gill as deputy minister, and requested Doctor Sahib to negotiate a compromise on their behalf. Doctor Sahib inquired, "Where is Pagal Seth?" I said that he had not come. He said, "So they sent you. Okay tell me, do you know what a deputy minister is?" I said, no, please explain. He said, "This is a deputy minister—a mudguard. The they pay you any salary?' Seething in a fit of rage, I had answered, 'No, they don't' and had walked away. No. Without money you do not associate with anyone. Not even with your own natural father... I could barely mask my tears.

Am perfectly fine... This has happened with me several times. If I hadn't gone to Mumbai then, I would surely have committed suicide. Would have been dead. My mental state was such at that time. I went off to Mumbai, to Lataji's. There were just two goals in my life: one was to meet Lataji and the other, to become a lama. I met Lataji. I feel honoured that I am among the few people whose phone number Lataji remembers, and that whenever I wish I can telephone her. I have the number to the phone in her bedroom. On my birthday she felicitates me. She suggested that I should come to Mumbai. That she will get me married. When I refuse, she says with affection that I am such a dolt.

mudguard can protect the engine from mud and muck. It cannot pull the train. Only the engine can pull the train." He gave such an example that he shut them up with his answer! He said, "Look, if you will take Meeha Singh Gill as a full-fledged minister, only then can we strike a compromise. Otherwise you can leave." They immediately agreed, all of them. You know, there are so many such incredible stories! At that time Doctor Sahib used to live in the 26 Alipore Road bungalow. We, too, stayed there for many days. We were so many of us. We were one team. But our community was unable to take care of its people. Now they are scattered all over like chaff in the wind... Now I, too, am ailing mostly. Even walking around is difficult!'

The Professor has heaved a cold sigh. After a stiff bout of trembling and shaking, PbhagMull has again become a bundle and withdrawn into his patchwork quilt.

The second goal is to become a lama. That is yet to be reached. I had gone to McLeodganj, where I ran into a lama of a very high calibre. That day it was mummy's death anniversary. I asked him to pray for my mother. He prayed. Then I told him of my desire to become a lama. He inquired about my original faith by birth. I said I belonged to Sikhism. He responded that this, too, was a holistic religious order, and that I should imbibe its virtues. 'No need to become a lama. Liberation can be achieved from there itself. However, if your heart does not agree, then come anytime...' Brotherji, his words made a deep impact upon my mind. What is more, the countries that follow the Buddha, there are amazing tales that are widespread about them, too. I had gone to Thailand. The cleanliness seen there was simply astonishing. Compared to Bharat, it is such a small country. But it is fully successful. It has few natural resources, so earnings are made out of tourism itself. You will find thousands of female sex workers standing by the

Retired Professor Jauhall's prattle

Look, the point is that the British gave us one centralised hukumat. *Because whoever the colonial ruler may be, he will sit at the centre of the nation and rule the entire* mulk. *The colonial raja cannot afford the luxury of scattering his raj about in different places, a bit here, a bit there. That same legacy we have inherited. Post-Independence, this has been our greatest tragedy. An example is the Soviet Union model, even though the Soviet Union had with it so many mulks and it had given them all autonomy, yet their governance was in the hands of the party—centralised! At that time a question had emerged. When Hindustan formed the colonial integrated centralised* roadsides. But they won't be ill or diseased like ours. You have to first ask them. If they are agreeable and consent, then it is okay. Otherwise the minute you tease them, the police will arrive. I had gone to Thailand. Incredible experiences those were. I shall tell you about them some other time. Had a lot of fun and frolic...!

Anyway, it is good that we have re-turned towards this turn in our talk. Now the need for liquor consumption, it seems, has attached itself to me as well. If we had continued in the family loop, then even the drinking of liquor would have turned sour.

constitution and implemented it, and thereby integrated all the states within it, the question that had raised its head then had also risen in the Soviet Union, and that was: what will you do with the bureaucracy? How will you control the bureaucracy? This question had triggered a lot many discussions amongst us. Then at long last the debate and discussions had ceased!

See, I have no other issue. It's just that my chetna *nosedives sometimes. Now, where was I? I'll have to be reminded. Actually my mother has just come to my mind. There is no one to take care of her. She does not get along with my wife. Which daughter-in-law gets along with her mother-in-law! I alone attend to all her needs. What else can I do? Now she must be itching to go pee, and I'm not around. She will not say a word to my wife. Then she will pee in her clothes. And until I reach home, she will continue to lie inert, as she is. My wife, too, will be sulking in her own cocoon. She just doesn't understand the problem. But she*

She, I, and space

Bloody hell, neither of the two will come into my grasp! Neither the hem nor the scarf of the matter can be grasped. The fingers clutch a few strands but then again, smooth as silk, the fabric slips. The two aren't that street-smart either. It's just that I am unable to figure out things. Actually there is no comparison between the body's alacrity and the mind's speed. The potential of the mind's speed cannot be achieved. It can beat the speed of light even. But even then, it is through the momentum of the

can't do much either; she has herself retired. She carries around her own weight with great effort. But what allergy ails her that my mother resists even the touch of her hands! No, no, I shall leave, have got to return and attend to mother. All right, if you insist, then we shall talk a bit more. Though, nowadays, there is no point in talking. Our intellectuals that are, they, too, have sold themselves.

Right, I was saying that the centralised governance that we have is bound to go corrupt in all likelihood. And along with it, also its largest bureaucratic structure—its structure of governance. Ditto was the state of the Mauryan sultanate. The Mauryans had a centralised form of governance. Their sultanate had collapsed under the weight of its own bureaucratic spread. That in itself had raised moot contradictions! What happened with us? We have inherited our legacy from the colonial system. It is not of our own choosing. That would have been the case if at body that it must be realised. Body language itself is attached to the mind's swing. Something or the other does emerge and lodge itself in the gaps. Now that day I had almost panicked into action. I had gone to meet her. She had made a joint programme with this friend of hers. This girl is half her age. Extremely beautiful. Like a rubber doll. A dollop of butter. In the sun she begins to melt. Honestly, I speak from experience. Her skin is like a rose in the sun, flushes pink and peach. Of heart, too, she is incredible. *Khush dill*, spilling with mirth. Her blooming countenance spills joy. But she hasn't got married as yet. There could be many reasons. That day we three went together to a restaurant. Then to a huge mall in the vicinity where we plunged into a shopping spree. They began to scout for footwear. We were in a tipsy jaunty mood. We two selected our respective pairs of footwear and quietly slipped out of the mall. The girl got stuck in there. And then she began to look for us inside. Standing outside, we kept laughing. When

the time of Independence the country were given the option of a party that was revolutionary in character. A party that was so detached from all the institutions of the English that at its very inception it would have flushed all of them out. And after flushing them out... Well, Gandhi was very clear that this kendriya satta, *this power at the centre, would surely do us all in one day. And that it should have been disintegrated. And that thereafter the villages should have been allowed to handle their own economies and walk with them, too! So they wouldn't have needed to turn to anybody...*

Please remind me, what was I saying? ...I tend to be forgetful. My mother, too, has the habit of forgetting. She has been given to forgetting right from the beginning. My father was absentminded, too. But he was a saint at heart. All his life he served the sadhus and fakirs. He did not worry too much over his family. ...Yes, please do remind me from time to time.

she finally emerged, she was bursting with anger. Her nostrils emitted sound bubbles of rage, phoon-phoon. We presumed it was a romantic sort of mock rage, but no, she was earnestly furious! This was terrible indeed; she couldn't even tolerate a joke. Trill-trill, her tears began to stream. We both went silent. She flung the sandals on the backseat of the car, quietly slipped into the driver's seat and started the ignition. For a long time her eyes continued to flow, trill-trill. Nobody uttered a word. We continued to sit in utter silence. The car, after meandering here and there, went and parked itself in front of her friend's house. It was a colony on the outskirts of the city, dense with trees. Here the darkness seemed to thicken somehow.

Her friend opened the gate and quietly planted herself behind it. From this one's nostrils the flaring sound of 'phoon-phoon' was now accompanied by the emission of steam; in place of tears, the eyes were now streaming blood. She had gone inside. This

...Okay, yes, so we were talking. Yes, we must acquaint ourselves here with the federal system. What is it in the federal system as it prevails in Amrica? Canada also has a federal system. They have different states. On top of those federal systems there is one central government. Twenty-one states are there. The states have law with them; they have finance; they have governance, all the paraphernalia of hukumattan. *The word hukumat comes from the Mughal context. But even the Mughal states got entangled in the bureaucratic wrangle. Their systems, too, went the same way. Is it that their banking system and methodology failed?*

The banking system followed by the federal government was also followed by the state governments. That system was either of the state government or of the private sector in which it was embedded—for their own profit—what Chomsky calls 'profit over people'. So the private sector that was theirs was in fact abetted one began to honk the horn loudly and repeatedly. When after a few repeated honks her friend did not come out, the horn began to blare continuously. I had come with her to a girl's house so late in the night. However intimate she might be with her, I was also aware that this intimacy of theirs was deplored by this girl's family. Her brothers are also very aggressive. For a brief spell my breath got hijacked. What a cursed place! The very thought gave me the jitters, but I lacked the guts to say a word to her. The horn kept on blaring continuously. Then when the friend came out, I got even more scared. Her face, however, was calm. It wasn't taut or stressed. I experienced some relief. She quietly opened the rear door and took her footwear. Then, softly saying, 'Take care', she went back indoors. This one drew in a deep sigh and reversed the car. I felt even more scared but thanked my stars. It was imminent to vamoose from the scene; the rest could be handled later. With her, there wasn't so much to fear, though. When we emerged from

by greed of profit; it inflated itself immensely like a balloon such that the balloon ultimately burst. That profit caused the inflation. What is happening in Bharat? Our legacy is a part of that centralised system of governance. You do not have to search for reasons for corruption as to why this or that happened, whether it was for this reason or that reason. These reasons are a part of the system. Why won't there be reasons?

Now there is one office. There is one deputy commissioner. The deputy commissioner is controlling the entire district. The senior superintendent of police, the block development officer, they are all working under him. He calls all the meetings, all the money comes to him and he alone distributes the funds to all. How did he become such an expert of everything? When you invest in one person, in a young man, such unlimited powers, then... Now, the Indian Administrative Service system was borrowed from the English. The English had made that system for their that colony, I spotted a car that seemed to be following us. When we slowed down, that car would slow down, too; when we picked up speed, that car would also accelerate. From a desolate road we had now reached a road bustling with traffic. The terror in the mind now began to abate. It seemed as though it had all been an illusion. However, I was still unable to muster the courage to talk to her or begin a conversation.

God knows what all had continued to simmer and boil in the heart. Yaar, this girl! She actually loves her. A masculine kind of love...with all the passion and vigour—as if she were her very own delicate, dainty sweetheart. She is scared of her inner man, though. Visions of the two of them in an intimate clasp began to tantalise my mind like on a video screen. But then, how did she get into a relationship with me? That girl knows of this as well. Otherwise she couldn't stand me either. Was stark jealous. However, when she meets me, a mere glimpse of me is enough to

own benefit and convenience. If the deputy commissioner is an Englishman, he would be brought in from England. These people took in that system as it was. Plato used to say, when you wish to appoint someone as an administrator, they should not be below fifty years of age. They should have in their possession complete maturity. Friend, now you make boys of twenty-five, twenty-six, IAS officers. You bring in a man of twenty-eight, twenty-nine and make him responsible for an entire district, give him the entire fund amount to handle, how will he not become corrupt? How will he not become so? Even if he is an honest soul, with all the means that are at his disposal, once he has assimilated all of them, they will eventually lead to the generation of corruption within him.

Bhai sahib, *I tend to forget from time to time. Please do help me remember. Now I forgot what it is I was talking about. Fact is that my wife is not at fault here, nor my mother either. The* set her abloom. This one is unable to figure it out. She once told me how, when she had suddenly met this girl for the first time, she had placed her hand on her thigh. Her hand had rested there for an eternity. It was just one brief silent spell. Merely an exchange, a give and take, of energy. There was no other movement then. Perhaps all thought had become suspended. However, we can't say for sure. Then suddenly this girl had given a startled tremor and clasped her in an embrace. And then she had slipped out of her arms. This one was consumed with desire. I was reminded of my first love. On the first occasion, that girl, too, had clung to my chest and stood clasped to me for such a long spell. Then she had turned scarlet with shame, I don't know why, and suddenly run away. With this one, too, the same thing had happened. Having located her address and whereabouts, she began to stalk her. Then she began calling her on the mobile. That girl would sometimes respond to her in the most civil manner, and sometimes she would

fault in fact is mine I suppose. Now, my children do not live with us. Well, they have a life of their own, why should they not enjoy it. They must enjoy it, when did I say they shouldn't. The fault is actually nobody's. The fault lies always with the system. It is we who settle into habits. And this we ourselves need to realise. I, for instance, have held on to my mother's hand, to wash her hand and help her with ablutions. Now that, my dears, is my discretion.

However, it is good that you have reminded me, I was talking about what happened sixty years later; matters which could have been debated upon fell silent. Nobody paid heed to the functioning of the bureaucratic structure and how it was to be controlled and managed, how issues of centralised funding were to be handled. Now, centralised funding, as you know, flows from the central government. From there it comes downwards. From where does it come, from the top. Now they have their own be mean and give her the slip. During this period, she used to speak to her or meet her sometimes; her feet would then traipse in the clouds. She would constantly chatter about her.

Today we had gone to the park. We sat on a narrow swing for a long time, and kept on swinging. That picture of Krishna-*Leela* which sits in one corner of her house, I see that picture turn a shade darker now. That picture which depicts Krishna performing *raas-leela* with village damsels, the *gopis*...thousands of Krishnas! The central scene shows him swinging with his beloved Radha on a *peeng*, a rope-swing slung from a tree. Then, when there would be no communication from that girl, this one would wear a long face and go into a sulk. Even with me she would break into a grump at the turn of every sentence. She would misinterpret every little issue and elicit from every word some twisted significance. Would pick up a fight for no reason at all. Those days I used to be quite scared of her. But to comprehend her is not in my capacity.

evidential logic that of the total rupees that are allocated for the projects, from that only fifteen–twenty paise are to be spent on the project; the rest is all gobbled up by middle men. How that project is shaping up, how is its survey being done, to whom is the money to be given, to this one and to that one, and then to the contractor as well...thus distributing-distributing the money like this, the project goes kaput. How can any development happen in this country if we carry on this way?

It so transpired that all our administrative offices that existed, they have collapsed. No system of any sort prevails. No work is being done either. You give the money and the work shall be done. Otherwise not. Well, if the work gets done even by giving money, fine. If it does not get done, then it never gets done.

Now, what happens is that even a regular, ordinary person they label as napunsak, *meaning, impotent and useless. Over time, with repeated usage, the fellow actually begins to believe*

Watching this relationship, trying to figure it out and assess it, four years had passed. During this period, I witnessed a lot. In the beginning, that girl had got into an alliance with a married colleague of hers. This one was extremely upset. She would argue with her. This one would expose the politics of it. That one would say, 'He feels lonely. His wife is insane. She does not understand him. He breaks down. Weeps. Takes to the bottle. He is my friend. I understand him. A friend is one who supports you and stands by you in your hour of need. I have to be his support! How dare you stop me!' She would blurt out all sorts of things. I kept cautioning her, however, not to abet this girl to such lengths. But this one was so indulgent with her that many a times it used to terrify me. This one would interfere in every matter of hers. To the extent of determining even the way the girl lived her life. She considered it her right. That one, too, would often behave likewise; but on many occasions it seemed like she had changed. I'd be driven into

that he is indeed a napunsak. Well, but we were talking of something else. Now consider the public sector, for instance. The public sector they put under the central government. All the units of the public sector are under the central government. All the appointments are made from there. Near our Ganganagar, in Suratgadh, there is a co-operative farm that was built with the Soviet Union's assistance. They procured thousands of acres of land and started co-operative farming on it. A retired DIG was appointed as its director. At that time we had challenged their decision: what is it that you are doing here? Why appoint a retired DIG here? Because the powers are with the central government, for any such position they appoint just about anybody they favour. You wish to appoint a high court judge it is the chief minister's will. He can induct an individual with just ten years' experience. He has the power to do so. This is the same thing that Noam Chomsky called 'manufactured consensus', which you a state of perplexity. Would attempt to understand the equation the two shared, but these two like slippery fish would slip through my hands.

Then that girl tried to bring her colleague to this one's house. During that period, I had observed that she was in two minds; emotions of fear and reserve would often play upon her face. Many ups and downs must have run through her heart. She wasn't talking openly to me either. She was merely roasting in a state of indecision. 'Yaar, that man has two daughters. Such an alcoholic, too; comes to office all drunk. To establish relations with such a fellow, what sense does it make? If his wife is such a fool then how come two daughters were birthed? Besides, what is *her* connection with his family matters! Now she has started bringing him over to my house. I feel scared, shit scared. Tomorrow if any hanky-panky were to happen, her family members would come looking for me. They already accuse me for having sheltered her...

people call representative, it is all manufactured in fact! With all that power the chief minister loses his balance. Now all the states there are, their chief ministers have all the powers with them. And yet none of the powers are with them. All powers are with the centre. Even at the centre, the prime minister has no powers. Who has the power? All powers are with the bureaucracy. Bhai, locate at least with whom the powers rest...? Take some decision, please. No decision is taken on any matter! So the money, the funds there are keep rotating, but no one knows who will decide for what!

Bhai, the old ones that are, they are often plagued by the problem of bawasir, *what you call piles or haemorrhoids. I, too, am troubled by it many a times. My wife is very often troubled by it. My mother, too, suffers from it. There is no cure for it either. For a long time now I have also suffered from high blood pressure. That is why I do not venture out so often. Even today*

If she desires to get married then she should go ahead and marry. To go around like this with someone who is already married... Talking about marriage, no one seems good enough for her... Sometimes I feel it would be better if this were to go through. This is imminent. If she goes through with it a couple of times, she will become normal. But why with this married man alone? She could go live with some young boy-shoy. Fall in love. I fail to understand her even one bit. She is causing me a lot of *dukh*...!'

The whole year round, some *khich-khich pich-pich* had gone on between the two of them. During that period, I had felt bewildered and scared, really scared. Heartbroken at her hands, this one would break into my arms, and as a result, my male ego would wax stronger. I would caress her hair. Lying in my lap she would sob like a baby. And I would drink her tears. Caress her body. By and by her fingers would entangle and play with the hair on my chest. She would drown in a pool of love. 'Many men

I could not have made it but then I thought, well, I'll get to meet some friends-shrends. But about these discussions I did not know that one would also have to talk. Well, never mind that. Yes, what were you saying? You had interrupted in between. No? Okay, I thought you were saying something. If you do not like it we shall stop here. We can listen to some other friend speak.

Okay, I shall try and wrap it up quickly. The issue was, who was taking decisions regarding the education system? Who was taking decisions about the law? When some bills come to the assembly for discussion, within ten minutes all four are passed. Nobody thrashes them, nobody studies them. Who has prepared the bills? The secretaries. Where do ministers have the time to examine or read the bills and see what is in them. No discussion happened on any one of them. No discussion takes place on any forum. That bill is to be made into a law; it is not some petty matter. That law must be scrutinised before it is cleared. The get their chest-hair shaven...', she would casually say. I would be stung by a serpent. Become hideous. The sensation is unlike that of being stung; it is more like humiliation. I would lose all self-awareness. Several days would pass like this.

Then suddenly that girl would land up in our midst. She would change a lot of things. She would get angry, court a sulk. And vent her anger upon me. This one would stutter and plead before her. Beg. Weep. Go down on her knees, place her head upon her feet. Honour every whim of hers. Waste thousands of rupees on her. Put morsels of food into her mouth and feed her. Fall ill in her illness. Breathe through her lungs and see through her eyes. Coalesced with each other, they were one, and I between them, would go into deficit. A beggar with a begging bowl. Then the both of them would turn their affection upon me. They would feed me this and sometimes that. A special meal would be cooked and served at night. I would be waited upon

entire education system we have received from the British. All our laws are of the British. All is of the British. Who were they? They were rulers. They used to rule in the colonial way. They had made a system with the purpose of defining how we were to be ruled and governed. They had formulated one law for Hindus; when we analyse that, we are able to get an insight into the dynamics of how laws were made. How they used to send two or three people to conduct surveys who would ask about what the laws of inheritance should be, what the divorce laws should be... so the ad hoc systems that prevailed at the time were eventually made into laws. Those very laws became for us a form of God's laws. And we have not even reviewed them.

Actually the moot problem that prevails is our colonial legacy. This colonial legacy is corroding our entire system. ...Yaar, this bawasir troubles like hell sometimes!

hand and foot. Fountains of trilling laughter would be unfurled. And all, all would be in a state of bloom. A film outing would be planned. Kurukshetra's lake, the Brahma Sarovar would cast its spell upon us. The Wagah border beyond Amritsar would call out to us. We would set out for a drive. Time would fly like crimson-coloured paint. Then she would run into exhaustion. I would express some desire of mine. She would oblige. And then revert to bitterness again. I would be dropped off by the roadside. These two would drive off into the distance. I would keep staring at the rear of the disappearing car.

Anyhow, nowadays that girl is fully involved with the son of some professor of this one. She has been spending nights with him. She has broken up with her. This one, too, after much grieving, has begun to look composed. But every gesture of hers has changed. She refuses to say a thing about her. She wants to put a lid on the chapter. However, she seems to be undergoing

...Now an army of those who had liberated the country has emerged. And this whole lot is eating up the pension. The security measures for all the prime ministers, ex-prime ministers, the expense for all these, from where does it come? We eighty crore people are spending. Twenty crore people are eating. We are drawing pensions and salaries, but we are doing nothing, we have no production to show nor is any work being done by us. Who is feeding us? The eighty crore is feeding us. We desire to keep that eighty crore in a state of suppression. What does our state do? It hegemonises that eighty crore with rods and batons. The farmer runs the plough, the mason makes homes for us, bakes bricks for us, day and night they are all slogging for us. Hungry as hogs they keep on working. At their expense we continue to eat and profit. We who are the thugs and thieves. Therefore, there is no need to worry or feel bad that we are soaked in corruption. The money moves among the twenty crore. They keep rotating it

immense trauma. To let go of the one we love is a very difficult task. But this one, it seems, wants to seal the separation.

'I've left her! It is a very difficult matter, I know. But she is now involved with that boy. And the longer she stays with him, the sooner it will become more and more normal. But I fail to understand her. Why must she get involved with married men alone? Her attitude towards women is based on a killer instinct. She will never once pause to think about the woman whose husband she romances with. I think contrarily. I tend to have immense sympathy for the wife—the other woman. This one does not think like that. Says, that fault lies with the other woman—for lacking an intense passion and the equipment to take care of her husband. "Or perhaps she cannot give him the love, the necessary sex, so then her man will naturally look for it elsewhere. I can give him more love, more passion. He will stay with me. I am more sexual. He wants to climax. I am that very climax." I object.

*among themselves. From within this circle someone purchases a car, someone a motorcycle. Someone gets pension, someone gets sixth pay commission. The matter is clear now that twenty crore people in Hindustan rotate all that money among themselves. Like there is news now that Ambani gifted his wife a cruise liner worth four hundred crores. Bhai, who are you? Now this is what we call the new economic order. This is Manmohan Singh's style of generosity—*udarikaran*! Udarikaran means that one person can purchase property worth thousands of crores. There is no accountability for anyone as to how is it that you are able to acquire so much property. How does it come? By the exploitation of people. The* karkhanas *where you get work done cheap from the labourers, all the profit comes to you while those labourers, utterly abused and misused, are toiling away. Who has permitted you to take maximum profit? Has our government given it? Fail the public sector and bring up the private sector!*

I'm not in agreement with her... But then, what is it to me? But then again, shouldn't I take the decision to end this? You only tell me what to do. This is a very traumatic time for me...'

I looked deep into her eyes and said, 'Yes, take it. Give her at last her "space"...'

'I do give her *her* space. But she merely wished to use me. Wished to make use of my home. She terms usage as space. I refuse to give her that "space". Do you think like her as well...?'

'No...no. I'm not saying that. But can you really let go of her? If you can, then let her take her freedom. That alone is her path. She needs a man. Leave her to her choices... Let fly. What is it with you! Leave her...!'

'Yes. That is why I say this. Now she has no time for me. Even when she used to call me in the middle of the night, I always had time for her. Now when I call her, she just cuts my call. Now since she lives with him, my calls will anyway cause her discomfort.

No, Bhai sahib, why do you bother with dinner? Food we can eat later. First let us finish the talk at hand; it is very essential. Right now the issue is more important, not rotti. Do not trouble yourself over food. However, today it is colder than usual. If a cup of tea could be brought, it would be nice. Okay, whatever you say. But if I could have some tea it would reduce the cold. I will be able to talk a bit better. Yes, some tea please.

So I was saying that the most significant issue at hand is that the kind of education system we have has rendered a majority of the population of Hindustan illiterate. Another point is that the children in the public schools, their minds are being shrunk, they are being made stupid. People are very perturbed by the word 'stupid' and feel that this word ought not to be used. I say stupid is a very mild word considering how charred I am, how bitterly exasperated I am. Bhai, by sending all your kids to public schools, you the middle classes have made them stupid. Taught them

She simply cuts them. Even to give ear to my words she no longer has the heart... to justify herself she has spread this rumour in our circle that madam does not give her space. Now what am I to do? She gives justification even for not answering my calls. She has now begun to say that a person needs to have some private time. So now she needs some private time... What about us? Don't we need private time, too? We stayed loyal to her all this while. But her privacy...!' She broke into tears.

I had breathed a sigh of relief. That she had at last stepped back from her a little. But from her swollen wet eyes it appeared as though she had gotten attached to her with renewed vigour.

English and cut them off from Hindustan. They do not know how wheat is grown. They do not know how corn is produced. They do not know what Hindustan is. What the culture of Hindustan is, what its sanskriti *is. It is from these public schools that your DCs will be made. These are the stupid fellows who are ruling. These public school fellows, their next generation has arrived and is ruling. All the rest are uneducated. Meaning, not a trace of what we call education has been left in this country. In this country corruption is not an issue at all. And what estimate will you make about the laws of this country?*

Five daughters were molested by someone. Next morning he will be bailed out, that is if he goes to jail at all. People are lying on the footpaths starving and stitchless. People have become brutal. Before the coming of the British there was no beggary here. How did these beggars come to be? What did we do to create this state of things? The gravest durdasha *and misfortune was that we*

An attempt to forget her

Yesterday our designer got married. Pretty good gathering there was at the wedding. After ages we had such fun! Didn't feel like drinking much either. Otherwise in the last few days, drinking had touched half-a-bottle. It would result in a total loss of consciousness. In the night all kinds of messages would get sent to female friends; next morning, however, attempts at a recall would fall on their head. Sent messages would be deleted that very instant, lest the gharwali should read them. And more, god

adopted the colonial legacy as it was. We kept digging deeper and deeper into that abject slavery and that misery.

Bhai sahib, the thing is not that a man cannot fall in love or that a man cannot transcend his gender. I did not say any such thing. It is possible that my father may have been androgynous, or that I may be. It can even be that the entire Punjab may be androgynous. It is even possible that it's just a figment of one's imagination. Oh, I see. That is why I was saying please keep telling me what it is that I was talking about. All right, I shall talk about the public sector only.

...Now the public sector was maligned. What happened? Look, now there is one more problem here, and that is when the country became free, the private capitalists who hailed from here, they did not have such large capital. On their own steam they could not build large manufacturing units. These are the ones who partnered with the government. They asked the sarkar to build

knows what all keeps rolling through the mind. At night I lose all discretion, such as, in the middle of the night one must not call an unmarried young girl. But what shall I do. She behaves so provocatively that I go into a torment. When she ran into me, she agreed to drink coffee. Then by and by she relented. Then at the spur of the moment she refused. Said, 'Erase that thought from your mind. I'm going to get married. Please... Do not even think about me. We are just friends as in earlier times. Wipe out the rest from your mind... Please!' I was flabbergasted. Nothing seemed right. I was unable to put a curb on the chaos within my chest.

What was this that had transpired? What made her change her mind in two minutes? I'd even agreed to her suggestion about 'limits'. That it would not be possible to go on a long drive, even to that I'd agreed. I'd agreed to every condition of hers. She had even accepted my first gift. Then this all of a sudden. This was unbelievable. Surely there was something that had caused this.

industries under the public sector. The government established industrial manufacturing units. The government became the capitalist. I mean the poonjipati. *It was not the public sector. It was the sarkar that became the poonjipati. With the government turning capitalist, twenty years later when our capitalists came to power and forged alliances with foreign countries and corporations, they did away with the public sector. They caused the fall of the public sector.*

Now then, it was not the small poonjipatis but the big poonjipatis that pushed their way up to prosperity. The banks that were nationalised, they fed the large capitalists. Once the large capitalists acquired the funds, they asked these banks to leave. Now we have no need of you. Now we are making our own banks. And what was the situation like earlier? They did not have the funds to lay an iron factory. They asked the government to please spend for them. The government spent the money. And of

But what? Why did she say yes initially? What kind of a 'behave' was this? My heart had gone bankrupt totally. I sent her a polite message as response. No answer. Then another message the night after, apologising for the message I'd sent the previous night. That in future a similar thing would not happen. She only responded, 'It's okay'. This 'It's okay' hit me like a bullet in the head. What kind of an answer was that? Yaar, such emotional coldness. She was too hard of heart. Though she did not appear to be so. Her eyes would generally remain moist. On the first meeting itself she had willingly come for coffee. Then what had happened now so suddenly? Yaar, I couldn't tolerate this.

One night I again began to send her messages. One, two, three, four, five, six...dozens of messages! She did not acknowledge any. Yaar, now why did I message her so repeatedly? You have broken my heart. You have broken my heart. You have broken my heart. You have broken my heart. You have broken my heart. You have

all that money, to whom did the whole profit go? To the private poonjipati. The advantage of the nationalised banks was reaped by the private capitalists. Now those wealthy people, the private capitalists, what did they need the public sector for? They kept it from being improved. It could have been improved, but no, it wasn't. What I am saying is, Bhai sahib, there is a bank. You are talking about corruption! People were burnt! Give a show cause notice to one person, saying, "Brother you came late, we are suspending you." Bhai sahib, for one entire year no person would dare come late. People in fact would come ten minutes early.

In Hindustan so many people are poor. People are in such dire need of employment. Look at all these offices. There is one office of agriculture. I said to its chief, expel one person, then you'll see who comes late! How will they not work! But he didn't, because he himself doesn't want to work. Why doesn't he want to work? Because there is a lack of incentive. Who has broken my heart. You have broken my heart. You have broken my heart. You have broken my heart. You have broken my heart. You have broken my heart. You have broken... Enough! But this was exactly my state on that day. And in this state of mind I had kept on sending her messages. I do not know what might have transpired with her. It is this very condition of the heart I was going to talk about.

Yesterday that designer boy's father had become emotional while dancing *bhangra* on the stage. My brother, too, had sobbed like that. So that the boy should not know of it, we had steered his father off the stage. I had been showering currency notes over his head. Then suddenly, I don't know why, he had become emotional. And burst into tears. I had embraced him. Like a child he had sobbed. What might have been in his heart one cannot tell. In my mind, his life story began to replay itself—it was a story that his son used to narrate often with much sentiment. He had

incentive? The deputy commissioner has it. No, even the deputy commissioner does not have incentive. Who has incentive? The minister has it. No, even the minister does not have it. It is with the prime minister. No, even the prime minister does not have it. There is nothing nowhere. All of it was planned so that no one has anything at all.

There is no transparency in anything. A question could be put before someone, before a DC, for instance, that in your district within a year, what all work was done? No one asks. Bhai, how did you distribute these funds? Meetings are called; no officer opens his mouth in his superior's presence. Bhai you gave away so much money to this department, for what? But he gave so he gave. No one will question the action. Is this some sort of charity that they dole out? Is this how charity is given? What would that chief minister have done here? He would have arrived, given a cheque of two crores to this one, five crores to that one... Bhai, abandoned his village much before he reached teenage. He would sometimes tell us that family members had thrown him out. I'd see a reflection of my own life story in his. The rest of it about being thrown out of the house I'd have guessed myself. I wondered how he had passed his entire life. With sheer hard work. He worked as a metalsmith, a *dhalaa-ee* who would melt metal, but he also sold vegetables. Milked cows. Got married. Fathered children. From a rented house moved to a house of his own. Got his kids an education. Got his daughters educated. Then came the phase of terrorism when being a brahmin became a curse. Surrendering home and hearth, he was compelled to come to Tarn Taran in Jalandhar. The household got uprooted. Desolation overwhelmed and consumed him. He began to remain unwell. His wife came down with arthritis. The daughters began to shoot up like bitter climbers. His heart began to quiver. The relatives in the native home abandoned him to cope with his troubles. Sometimes, he

what are you? Who are you? Bhai, you have offices, will the offices decide on their own who has to be given how much? Are you deciding what is to be given and what not to be given? All of this has been taken care of by the private capitalist. That is why he wants to overlook the corruption. He does not wish to stop it. Corruption does not exist. You tell me how can corruption proliferate? You cannot get a person arrested. That is not possible. The entire system from bottom upwards is yours. You do not need these offices. You do not want improvement in these offices. You do not need the department of agriculture either. In fact, you have no need at all! You say that it's okay, carry on eating money. Make merry! I mean, so then where will all this bribe go? It will circulate among the twenty crore people who will share the booty.

The matter of corruption is like this. The government schools you have shut down. We do not see this corruption at all. The would sit by himself and weep. His son would wipe his tears. This gave courage to his heart. Then by and by, the day of his son's wedding arrived, and then as he danced and danced, Brotherji suddenly went phuss and again broke into tears! I continued to hold him in an embrace.

Pbaaji, my elder brother, too, had wept the same way. It was at the wedding of his *Sali*, his wife's younger sister. We, too, were invited. We all had gone. From my in-laws' side, my own Sali and her husband had also been invited. We all were present there. My brother's father-in-law *sahib* is no more. His mother-in-law, too, is of delicate health. His brother-in-law is called Sindra. When Pbaaji got married, his two sisters-in-law were very small. Now they both were being married off. During the *vidaee*, the farewell ceremony, as the sisters turned to leave for their new homes, Pbaaji began to weep with loud sobs. I consoled him, but he was inconsolable. And I wondered how he would cope when his own

teachers that are there in these schools do not teach. They do not teach for the reason that the son of the sarpanch *studies in a public school. The sarpanch is in no need of this government school. He says, teach if you wish, don't if you don't wish, go have a blast! So all their incentive is killed.*

... And what is the media? Poor things all of them! The media is nothing at all! I am telling you, the Punjab state in itself is nothing. What does Punjab have? There is nothing in Uttar Pradesh. None of the states have anything. All the funds are with the centre. The centre is supposed to disburse all the funds. How does the centre disburse them, who disburses it, how, what does it disburse? Nobody knows anything. The secretary has put his signature, let the money be given. But given where? In the colonial rule that was, no system had been put in place. Even then it was hukam *from the top. Even now it is hukam from the top.*

daughter would leave home? After all, what was it that was in his heart? It does not happen that you marry off the girls and weep so uncontrollably. So much crying? This was the limit. I was unable to fathom my brother's heart. Thereafter I always perceived him as the pusillanimous sort. But that day when he wept, many other sorts of scripts had gotten etched upon my heart.

That same evening, with my Sali and her husband riding pillion behind me on my motorbike, I had come to the city. My Sali, who had sat in the middle, had dug her breasts into my back. Like the nails driven into the palms of Jesus Christ. From my heart my weeping brother's image, which had hung like a picture of Jesus Christ, had vanished. Instead, visions of an absurd sort had now begun to gallop in my mind. The nails were firmly plugged into my back. A sweet-sweet pain had emerged. What had happened thereafter I retain no consciousness of. By which route I had reached home even that I could not recall.

No issue is rationalised at all. No issue makes any difference to anyone at all. There is no logic behind anything. No justification is offered for anything.

However, what happened as a result of this? Here, the big capitalist is making money. He wants the system to continue as it is. Ambani and other such big capitalists are earning big time out of this same mess. They do not desire to correct this. We think it is not in their hands—no, actually, they do not want to see this corrected. So people like Manmohan Singh go around being prime minister. It is they who are consuming the real wealth. Gobbling it up. Their own people are sitting in the parliament. It is they who get the bills passed. Now see for yourself, what happened to insurance? The life insurance scheme was doing quite well. In fifty minutes they got a bill passed pertaining to insurance companies. No one came to know of it. BJP wanted it.

Yes, thereafter every time that my Sali sat pillion on the motorbike, the nails would get plugged into my back. Of their own volition. They had established their place. Quietly. Without any fidgeting, without any vulgar prompting. As though that were their most natural place to which nobody ought to have any objection or feel perturbed or disgusted about. I, too, had surrendered my back to them. I do not know how all this continued. But the sensation that prevailed was neither questioned by me, nor ever acknowledged by her.

Then one night, in my in-laws' house, my Sali and I were thrown together by chance. By then she was married and had delivered a son as well. We were accommodated in the sitting room on two adjacent folding beds. We slept off. There was no one else in the sitting room. From my nostrils the breath heaved and hissed phoon-phoon. In my back the nails dug in. Under the pretence of slumber I flung my arm upon her bed. My fingers

So BJP also supported them. The MPs were their own, purchased and pocketed in advance. The MPs were made by them. To them they dole out hefty funds. The MPs are theirs only.

...In the midst of all this mess, the capitalist who hails from here, he adds different shades to the picture. What happens is that the higher castes of Hindustan—this aspect we must specially keep in mind that we forget the issue of caste so many times!—the higher castes partnered with the Mughals and licked off the cream. Then they sided with the British and again licked off the cream. Now they are licking the cream by partnering with Amrica. Now if anyone is challenging them, it is the terrorists. They come and climb upon their five-star hotels. This new reaction is capitalism's very own progeny. An offshoot, it is the bastard son of that same reaction. And it is he who will also commit patricide. He has already assassinated the father. Who has birthed it? Terrorism is an offspring of this. He will also

touched her hair. I gathered a little more courage and withdrew my hand. After a while I aimed again. This time my hand landed in the right place. I left my hand unstirring right there. No movement. Then the hand was withdrawn again. Then she got up. I thought she might have gone to the bathroom. But she did not return. In my mind several questions began to spin. Did she realise what was coming? Or perhaps her boy lying with her mother had woken up. She must have gone and lain with him. But she might have thought that I had purposely... But I had acted in full assurance. Then why did she not return? I did not dare to even get up and look. But all night I was unable to sleep.

Then the next day I returned. During a conversation with my wife, I got to know that Sali was three months pregnant. I was shaken...!

die by it. His five-star hotels it will kill. When there is an attack on a five-star hotel, the newspapers scream that it costs twelve thousand rupees a night there, so then people say the buggers should have been killed anyway. People feel why were they spared at all? When there was an attack on the parliament, people said the bloody SPs should have been killed. People have become so alienated. They have become so divided, so disillusioned!

As someone was saying, where is my village? Where is my desh*? Where am I? What am I? Who does not ask this? That in the same Mumbai where thousands of people sleep on the footpaths, that in that same city there should be five-star hotels? From all this... Look, these people do not intend to finish corruption. They wish to see these public offices collapse. And collapse they will, and the powers will go into their hands. Where there is no logic, no justification, where no one is heard, it makes no difference. This amounts to the fact that there is no one to stop them. Every*

You won't find the dear lost ones

Yaar this *balaa*, this trouble has for no reason flung itself upon me! And there is no way I can figure her out. Many a times she begins to appear insane. For god's sake, can't you comprehend other people's compulsions! Why keep on piling and imposing on the other your own good self, that, too, when the other does not desire it and nor have you any close or distant relationship with him? Her father is an old journalist. At least with him there used to be a passing acquaintance. He goes around negotiating

person is then surrounded by corruption. Every person becomes insecure. They wish it to be so, that every person should become insecure and live in fear. If some person is eating money he will be fearful. Anxiety-ridden. The system breeds insecurity, it conspires to make one believe that he needs lakhs of rupees for his son's college studies. They have hemmed in the middle classes. They all are living in fear. Therefore the entire office is in fear. What corruption does is that it spreads angst. This same angst they wish to generate. What is there to lose? This is excellent. This is exactly what they want. For them the system has become paradisiacal, and for us crores of people, a living hell.

...Well, in the beginning the people wanted a change. They said, let all the institutions of the British be shut down. What was Gandhi's vision? This is exactly what he was saying, you leave our country and go, we will see to things by ourselves. Gandhi's vision was all right, but he did not know enough about the public

old age homes. Each to his own. Well, I thought he is needy, so let's help him. He shared the matter with her. She simply added more knots to it. Now I am a troubled man. I don't know what all she keeps telling and asking my wife. Among journalists all the gossip that does the rounds around me she keeps dribbling it into my wife's ears. On top of it she will say, 'I have full faith on Brotherji. He cannot be of that sort. It is these journalists that are so cheap. They fabricate all the gossip for sheer fun so that a colleague who is progressing, his feet can be squashed.' Really, who knows with how many of them she is on intimate terms! There are several confidential matters of my department of which even I am unaware but which she goes and reveals to my wife. When my wife asks me about them, it gives me the jitters. At times one is driven to exasperation at one's own foolishness.

One day when I returned from office, my wife beams at me and says, 'Today I'm going to give you a surprise.' I could not

psyche, nor was he aware of the historicity of the country's caste system. He was not able to enlighten the people. The reason he was not able to enlighten people was because he had with him 'Raghupati Raghav Raja Ram'. *He was in possession of Raja Ram. Gandhi did not wish to make a political force out of the Dalits of this land. That is how he felt and he got stuck among the upper castes. He was unable to implement his vision because the majority of people in Hindustan are Dalits. Gandhi did not wish to separate the Dalits from the mainstream. Ambedkar was open to letting them go their own separate way. Ambedkar wished to see the formation of a Dalit political force that would take the power of governance in their hands! Because they are more patriotic. They have love for this soil, because the bread that they eat comes from this very soil. The higher class does not eat its bread from this soil; they go off to Amrica. They actually sell their own country. They barter it.*

comprehend. As I put my bag down, she went into the kitchen and emerged with her, 'See, Diksha didi has come!' I mentally hit my forehead in vexation, and casually asked her how she was. That was enough to set her off. Don't know what she was fed at birth! A true daughter to her father, she yapped unrelentingly. Actually, one cannot even call her her father's daughter. Nor can one call her her mother's daughter, for had she been dear to the mother, would she have abandoned her when she was just six months old and pushed off with someone else? The mother had gone off with her lover. Or one could say she left because she was fed up of this one's father. Fed up not because of the beating and bashing, but because of his dark habits. She never turned back. After a long time, they got to know that she lives in Batala. By then this one, too, had got married and had in her lap a baby girl. This silly girl, hungry for her mother's love, or call her crazy, went off to meet her. That one refused to even recognise her.

They get money from the capitalists. They get money from foreign countries. Sitting abroad in a foreign land, they invest money in share markets. Wealth that they have received from the Mughals! Did the Dalits ever forge an alliance with the Mughals? No, it is the Rajputs who forged an alliance with them! This upper caste always fishes out of selfish motives. Out of selfish motives it partners with power. And when it fuses with the ruling powers, the Dalit is compromised. Satta *becomes strong. It is a trait of the higher castes that they always stick with the powerful. This is a chief trait of the brahmins and their* brahminvad. *Fact of the matter is that no war has been waged with the brahmins. In the Poona Pact, they killed Babasaheb Ambedkar. After the Poona Pact, Ambedkar just did not rise. We shall not discuss Ambedkar's Poona Pact here. Because we took advantage of the reservation clause. And Ambedkar was* not *in favour of reservation of this*

Instead she packed her off to the police station on charges that this girl was blackmailing her. After telling me about this on the phone for ten minutes, she had continued to weep. I, too, had wept with her. Then I had felt angry, with her or with myself I do not know. Perhaps with my wife, for she has given her a lot of space. Says, she is so sweet. In the face of her rationale, I had lost my guard. She had said, 'Look, I, too, need someone with whom I can share my heart. This poor thing is alone, too. The father is crazy. Keeps drinking. Didn't make a home either. Now he keeps knocking at the doors of homes and ashrams for the aged. With me, too, who is there? No in-laws, no maternal family either. The way my mother kicked me out of the house, that day I alone know what I faced. In all my life I shall never turn towards her...ever. Plus she then saddled me with the upkeep of this Buddhi tarr-tarr. As long as I continued to give them her pension, I was good, and he, too, was good. This time around the Buddhi refused them, so

kind. He used to say they will all get sold, they will die. Those people will buy out these folks. How many posts were reserved—ten or eleven. Ambedkar did not want this.

What the state did is that it trapped the Dalits into political reservation. Their commitment lies with the Congress, the BJP or with their own party. It is not with the Dalits, is it? When I questioned the MP, he said, "We need to talk about the party". But they do not allow us to. Just see the spectacle for what it is! Does anybody talk about it? Tell me, who was Kashi Ram? He was a very strong man. An incredible man, indeed. But when the upper castes acquire money, they get a man killed! Look here, a huge section of the Dalits was raised by the parties post-Independence. But in his last days, Ambedkar used to weep and wonder: what was this that happened? What was the future of the Dalits in this country? Ambedkar himself could not win. Because they—their minds—were terribly scorched and in flames. Now if she desires to help me, they are provoked—serpents slither on the floor of their chests. I have determined now that when the Buddhi expires, even then I shall not call them! Let them leave me now, and later face the consequences of abandoning me...!' And then with a sob she had burst into tears. I could not think of anything. Since a month now I have not been able to pull her out of mourning. For this very reason she began to lapse into unrestrained expressions of grief. Continues to grieve. Paral-paral her tears spill in streams. She keeps bad health. Tends to feel giddy. And her BP is low as well. Perhaps this one has come here to inquire after her health.

I wish to go past them. On the pretext of fetching a book I have gone off to the *chaubara*, the room on the terrace. My wife's words, 'When this Buddhi tarr-tarr expires, even then I shall not call them!' continue to spin in the mind. Will this Buddhi ever die?

a party of Dalits could not be formed. A republican party was made, but it failed. Then the Bahujan Samaj Party was formed; that, too, failed. They got the person kidnapped overnight. Because the Poona Pact was, I say, a turning point in the system of Hindustan. It's just that Ambedkar got fooled out of it. If only he had said that if my Dalits fight, they will die, too. The threat was that people of the higher castes would get them killed. They should have left them to die! I don't know what kind of pressures Ambedkar faced that he succumbed to Gandhi's urging. And what did Gandhi do? He went on a fast unto death! Do you really mean to say that he did not know what was happening? That he did not know what the implications of the pact would be or what consequences would emerge? How can you raise the Dalits? How can you establish a movement of the Dalits? ...So the crux of the matter is this: if you really want to know what truly happened

Do old women die? No. No, they do not die. I look around here and there. From a palatial house I look towards the terrace of the fourth house. Their daughter-in-law is sitting in one corner. What is she doing sitting there at this hour? She is eavesdropping on her father-in-law and mother-in-law who are conversing below. Ditto! The volume and tone of their conversation is audible even to me. No, that is not the daughter-in-law but the mother-in-law's mother-in-law. Yes, it is the daughter-in-law's grandmother-in-law, that is, her *dadi-sas*. Or perhaps the mother-in-law's mother-in-law, too, has a mother-in-law? They say that spirits of the aged continue to haunt and roam around the house. That their grandson can see the phantom spirits. He breaks into a sweat in the middle of the night, bawls loudly. Screams. He does not stop until he has awakened the entire street and raised a storm. To get him treated they have gone to so many places, but it has changed nothing. Yes, it is some old crone. I feel scared. I hurry back downstairs.

with the Dalits, then the entire political system, the history of Hindustan must be rewritten and retold from the point of view of the Dalits.

> Danda: Shastrit praja: sarva danda evaabhi-rakshit. Danda: Supteshu jagrit danda dharma vidu-burdha:
>
> *O monarch! It is* danda *that rules, regulates and restores the citizenry; when all living beings are lost to slumber, it is* danda *alone that keeps vigil; for this very reason the pandits signify* danda *as* dharma *and discourse upon it.*
>
> Dharma samrakshate dandasta-thaishartha naraadhip. Kama samrakshate dandastri-vargo danda uchyate.
>
> *O Rajan!* Danda *is the sole protector of* dharma *(righteous action), in the same way it protects* artha *(economy); and* danda *it is that protects* kama *(lust). From this premise itself,* danda *acquires the tripartite title of* trivarganaam.

When I come down, this one starts off with the same old tarr-tarr, tarr-tarr. She chatters more than the old hag! In a shrill voice of the most unpleasant sort! If you keep listening to her voice, you cannot match it with her visage. Even her anatomy is cast in a different mould. I had heard her speak on the telephone, and the impression it had cast upon the mind was of someone quite grotesque. But she is beautiful to look at. Even her hair is so beautifully styled. Height is middling. A slender, well-proportioned body. The eyes are splendid. Meaning, she is beautiful; to look at her more deeply, I wouldn't dare. I'm unable to attend to her words, but listen one must.

'Brotherji, they had left little me in a hostel attached to a school here in Jalandhar itself. My father as it is was a waster. My Chachis, the wives of his brothers, used to detest him. They used to detest me as well. For a long time, until I reached adolescence and became aware, I wasted away in hostels here and there. Then

Dandeta rakshyate dhaanyam dhanam dandena rakshyate.
Etaadvi-dwannu-paadatsva svabhaavam para-lokikam.

What more shall I say, the wealth and wellbeing of citizenry and all else they possess, is safeguarded by danda *(revenue) itself. O Rajendra! Deduce from this and resolve to decree* danda *as the watchdog of all citizenry. And deign to gaze on other worldly themes.*

—Shanti Parva

in Jalandhar itself I acquired a friend. She was my roommate. Not just roommate but also my destiny's mate. Her mother, too, had left her with her father at a very tender age, and eloped with someone else. Halfway through the nights she, too, would break into sobs. I used to hug her tightly and sleep. When I sobbed, it would be her turn to embrace me tightly. We were a great support to each other. Then we got separated. She went in one direction and I in another. Neither of us knew a thing. Then I began searching for her. On the basis of the conversations we used to have, I drew a map and went around, searching. But she could not be found. Many of her relatives behaved very nastily towards me. But I will certainly find her. I have pledged this to myself in my heart...!'

I wish to research this tendency to search that is in her. Why does she set out searching? Earlier she went off in search of her mother. Then she went searching for her father. Says her great grandmother is alive, where she lives she does not know but she will search her out for sure. Now with the matter of this friend, too, she got carried away. When my wife had given her directions to our house over the phone, she had said just give me the house number, I will search it out. Today she searched it out as well. When I asked her, she said, 'I found it very easily'. I was amazed, because many friends of mine, who have come here five–six times, still return without locating the house sometimes due to the twisting, turning lanes that lead up to it. Then they often request me to come rescue them. But I do not desire to venture out. I feel safe. Now she had found it in minutes. You are great indeed, Madam!

Wrap it up quickly, *yaar*

I knew that this firework would burst someday or the other. And yet like a pigeon I had kept my eyes shut. Actually I'm unable to tolerate anything of gross or fantastic dimensions. The veins of my brain begin to tauten. Now after hearing this news, I nearly went insane again. I'm being nasty and vicious to my wife. I knew it earlier as well. But her very condition had appeared to be such. Sister would announce each time she visited us, 'Now his condition has worsened far more. You know there are young girls in the house'. They are my *Jeth*'s, my elder brother-in-law's daughters and daughter-in-law. 'And he, towel wrapped around his torso, keeps wandering, sometimes here and sometimes there. Even begins to roll on the floor!'

'Have you taken him to some knowledgeable, wise person? What does he say?' I myself don't trust any special wise one, but this is how I question my sister all the time.

'What will he say...? Says your Jeth is haunted by some childless barren. His Taya, that is his fraternal uncle, had passed away, you know. And then this old crone called Akki was sent to my father-in-law's. Their business used to run well. Her family from her mother's side said never mind, our girl will be comfortable. But how were they to know that the frost would rain hard upon us and that they would be avenged. Then we got a shamanic *dhalaan* done for him so he'd be safe from black magic. Even then he did not recover. Then we approached another wise one. You will be astounded to hear that he came into our hovel and plucked earthen lamps from its nooks and corners as if out of thin air! He declared, "Your house is haunted by Baba Jinda Shah! Make space for him herein. Bring forth the pestle he used for pounding bhang, bring the wooden *khadanwan* he wore on his feet and the *langot* cloth he wrapped around himself, and place it all over here. Pray to Baba, make a wish. Feed four souls. Only then will you find release". We followed all of his instructions. We had to repeatedly light *chirags* in that nook till late in the night. Sometimes we would pick up the chirag and take it to the tombs in the graveyard. Really, these matters are so beyond one's comprehension.'

And today itself matters have climaxed to a point beyond limit. *Hudd hi ho gayi.* It is three days since my brother-in-law left home. First he said he'd return by himself. But since he didn't return, the matter has been brought to me. I am scorched. The tautened veins of my brain threaten to burst. I don't know why I did not get him treated earlier. With thirty-six doctor friends at my disposal, any one of them would have treated him and without charging any fees. Or I could have taken him to the civil hospital. But no, where do I find the free time. If I had that sort of time, wouldn't I have gotten the little ones' birth certificates done? It fills them with despair. My wife has taunted me a hundred times over it. Even the school people insult her.

Now who knows which way he might have gone? Will have to call the policewalas. Will have to get an affidavit made from the court. How will I put up with the sight of my weeping sister? And even if I do put up with it, how will I negotiate with the police guys? They interrogate you so grossly that... Well, let us see.

How lonely must the moon be on the rooftop of night

'Make an affidavit for a missing person, from Krishna... Yes, he is her husband, his name is Jinder... Yes, father's name is Rulia-Ram, village is Tarad and Fakh Khanna Lambda. Yes the district is very much Jalandhar and the tehsil as well. All right *ji*. Yes you may write, two days back. His mental state is not good. He has been ill for a long time... No, no treatment has been ongoing from anywhere. He was just taking treatment from random doctors here and there... You know what the state of the poor in the villages is. Consider this person's state: last summer, water in the taps had dried up. It's been a year now and they haven't been able to afford the charges for sinking the hand-pump deeper into the ground. They fetch water all the way from Ravidas gurudwara, which is at a distance of about two miles. They herd and take the cattle daily towards one pond, even at the risk of them falling ill.

But even in their suffering they do go off somewhere. Who will pull water out of the temple and give it to them! Yes ji, they are our relatives. But who has the time these days to take care of other people's matters! Now that this trouble has descended, I only have to run in all directions! Yes ji, when he left home, there were slippers on his feet. He was wearing pants of a light blue colour. White shirt and over it a torn, soiled sort of sweater.'

I have lost my courage. In case the corpse is brought for post-mortem or if there is an inquiry, then how will this tally? My sister had said that all he had wrapped around him was her *dupatta* and over it a frayed shirt, other than that, nothing else. But if I get this recorded, I dread the response it might elicit in the police station. They will summon my sister here. 'You must have been harassing him!' they will say. Thereafter a bizarre sort of parade would begin for his identification. Then would follow a discussion on swear words used by my brother-in-law. 'Hmm, so he used foul language, eh? You live with some so-and-so? Or you must be living with some other fellow!' And then one doesn't know what else... So ultimately the word 'live' would drag my sister into the torchlight of suspicion. No. No. But my heart says if she does 'live', then that is pretty much good. After all, friend, she has some needs, too. Does she not need to 'live'...!

'Yes, ji...! Yes, yes. Please write, ji. Height six feet, tall and well built. Colour of eyes, black. No scar on any body part. Yes he has a mole on his left cheek. A large heart. His hair is trimmed. Age, he is not forty yet. ...Yes they marry them off early in the villages. What else! What lifestyle can a poor man have, ji? Now he is so handsome the very sight of him makes one hungry!'

What sort of a visage will his be? The hair have become rope-like, they stink. Even the beard has grown hoary and stringy. From the beginning, his eyebrows have always jutted out straight and thick, they look quite gross. Now who knows what might have happened. With just a stole wrapped around his torso, who knows if it has stayed in its place or fallen off somewhere! God knows who all he might be begging from and eating. Or he might not be eating at all. Might have shrunk by now and become thistle-thin. And who knows, people might have taken him to be a *masat* and begun to worship and serve him! Sister did say that often people who walked past brother-in-law would genuflect in his direction as they went. Well, didn't he always say that Babaji visits him?

Yes! Like our village buffoon, that Lala. People might have taken brother-in-law to be a holy man, a *bhagat*. Who knows, they might all be at his service by now. I had gone to the village yesterday and had run into the Lala. He was in very bad shape. He had looked at me through his yellow saucer-like eyes and said, 'So you have become a *pardhan*, Lala! Pardhan of Ravidas gurudwara! Now you should make it effortlessly out of here. You'll soon get a visa! Tony has not returned yet. He has travelled afar...very far. That beanstalk would keep hitting the pardhan!' Lala's words were like pins pricking my heart. Tony's expression was eternally etched upon my mind.

Tony used to study with me. Their beanstalk of a father had kept busy all his life, overseeing labour welfare at a cold-storage plant. He'd draw deeply from the hukkah and keep saying something or the other in a loud voice to the labourer girls sorting potatoes. Many a time I, too, would accompany them for potato picking. There, among the labourers, amazing relationships used to develop. Many girls and wenches would reach there from the camp. During my class ten holidays I'd gone for a day with Tony. One girl there had become a sister to me. I wonder now what intentions might have stirred in that girl's heart. Tony and gang used to keep scouting round the area where the girls used to go to pee. The father would say nothing. Then hell had broken loose on this family. The elder brother who used to live in the colony suddenly passed away. He had left behind him four young daughters. The grief of his son was yet to abate when their mother Preeto, too, passed away. A long illness ate up their widowed sister. Then within a year's time some deadly disease ate up Tony! The sight of the grieving old beanstalk was more than one could endure. The entire village was shaken by the catastrophe. Calling out to Tony, Lala had wailed loudly! I, too, had wept with him. My mother used to tell me that we were born on the same day. Our midwife, too, had been the same. I was born two hours after Lala. That same night in the house of the Lambdas, a girl had been born. Her midwife, too, was the same as ours—from Amron. Later that girl used to study with me. She was exceedingly pretty. I used to keep touching her body, but only through the fingers of the midwife.

'...Yes ji! I shall get Krishna's signature on this over here. Yes ji. Yes ji. Never mind. I shall go to Lambde and return. It is okay ji. You tell me, how much is the fee? What shall we do, now how much expense can we really afford. You have no clue how home expenditures can run. Even the middle classes live hand-to-mouth. What else? Well, expenses that have to be borne will have to be borne, like it or not. Yes ji, yes...I shall get the signatures. Alright ji. Many thanks to you.'

Tears in brother's eyes

'Look here, earlier, women never joined in with the shouting of Veer Bajrangi's slogans and *jaikara*. Nowadays women singers shout Bajrangbali's shibboleths. He was a *bal brahmachari*—what do these women know! They are all lunatics! Women are not to shout shibboleths for Veer. Now you better look into this yourself...!'

I am amazed at the amount this barber knows. Totally bewildered. On the cable one Baby Rekha was singing Hanumanji's *bhet*. First she shouted the slogan, '*Jaikara e Veer Bajrange! Har Har Mahadev*!' This one responded to her with another slogan and a repartee to go with it. A weird guy is he. I desist from acknowledging him too much because he does all kinds of crazy things. God knows what all he keeps mumbling all the time. Some hocus pocus, as a Doabi would say, '*Ugg diyaan ptaal!*' His elder used to be a good man. Fat and round, nice and plump. Eyes deep red. Small delicate ears. Sparkling marbled eyes. Of middling build. What a spectacular old man he was. He has not been seen in a while now.

This is weird—I am staring at the very same gentleman's garlanded picture, and yet am unable to figure it out. 'When did this Babaji pass away?' I ask the barber. He looks at me in some consternation and says, 'Since when do you know him?' Even more incredulous now, I counter, 'Why?'

'Because he is my *lakkad-dada*! This portrait of his has been preserved by my ancestors. This is a painting, not a photograph. One of our ancestors was a painter as well. This painting of my great-great grandfather is in fact a family relic from very early times. My father's face is quite similar to his. You were perhaps talking about my father. Oh look at this, brother—this is his picture. It is now three months since he passed away.' I look closely—the visage is identical. I look at the eyes. His eyes, his face are the same. His son's as well. The grandson's eyes, too, are like his only. Suddenly the entire shop stocked with scissors and combs seems to be filled instead with pictures of the garland-wearing man. I get a bit scared. 'Phew!' The barber has run the blade in, through! Perhaps he has taken fright, too!

'What is this that you've done?'

'Never mind, I shall apply some *phatakree* on it. This in fact is a *dadree*, a clump of blisters that you have got here. My grandpa used to make and supply the medicine for this. I shall give you that same preparation. You must apply it. Only fifty rupees you have to pay me for it. That's all. Then just watch—in two days the dadree will disappear! It'll be a miracle, brotherji. You will be amazed. I swear by the jaikara—Veer Bajrange! Har Har Mahadev! Sorry! I don't know how this shibboleth slipped out of me and fused with the chanting!'

These shopkeepers should take care of their customers. They should not raise slogans at such loud volumes. And if they must indulge then they should first take the client's permission. This one, too, has pitched his voice so high. The one singing the hymn is completely out of tune and has no rhythm whatsoever. She is intolerable. Baba Harivallabh was once returning from somewhere. He was a *darvesh* musician. A sublime singer. A maestro of *shastriya sangeet* and the *dhrupad* form. He was to reach the Devi Talab Mandir in Jalandhar. He hired exclusively for himself a *saalam* tonga, a one-way ride, for the sum of two rupees. With a flourish the *tonga-wala* swirled his staff; we call it *shenta*. Now the horse began to canter. They had only travelled a short distance when Babaji asked the tonga-wala to stop the tonga. The tonga stopped. Babaji alighted. Giving two rupees to the tonga-wala, he said, 'You go back. I shall go walking by myself.' The tonga-wala, was bewildered. He caught hold of the darvesh's feet and pleaded, 'Babaji, what mistake did I commit?' Babaji raised him up by his shoulders and said, 'Your mistake there is none. In fact it is your horse that lacks a sense of rhythm. If the skewed cadence of her feet continues to fall upon my ears, I shall go berserk. Therefore I have gotten off.'

I feel disgusted with myself. Why did I suddenly begin to weep? The barber, too, got startled and has been staring at me bittur-bittur. But my tears are simply streaming away of their own accord.

'Never mind...never you mind... The patriotic sentiment is such that it overwhelms one. It happens. Even the narration of a heroic tale, if you look closely, is steeped in the *karuna rasa*. Laxman's separation from Ram brought tears streaming to the eyes of the great Bajrangbali as well. Heroes like them wept, too. We mortals are anybody's water-bearers. Brotherji, these singing bards are also incredible! They can melt a person like wax, by god! It is an incredible sight to witness. Har Har Mahadev. Bolo Shankar Bhagwan ki jai!'

The bhet singing of hosannas to the goddess has finally ceased. I am relieved. Glad to be rid of it. I don't know what happens to me. There is somewhere within a deep, deep gash that sometimes bursts open. Then the weeping is unstoppable. What is this that makes me lay my head in my wife's lap and weep away all-all night, I fail to fathom. She keeps running her fingers through my hair. And I keep weeping and weeping.

'Brotherji, clean up the hair from your armpits.'

I quietly remove and hand over my shirt.

'Raise your arms now, that's all.'

Arms raised, I stand thus as though being punished by the master!

The women consent

'Yes ji...why do they bellow so, these herds on herds? Why do they keep bellowing so...! A perpetual gaaw-gaaw-gaawing runs through the head. They climb down from the exit side and from the exit side they enter... A tremendous chaos...they cause such a hullabaloo! Gaaw-gaaw-gaaw...sounds bellow day night and day...! We are carefree people ji...look, we do not hit anyone with pestles...nor verbally abuse people...we just live in our own bubble. We prefer to beg and eat. We smoke our tobacco rolled in leaf. Hear hear...! How loudly they bay and bawl on so...!'

My brother-in-law is responding to the doctor's questions. He is in a very shattered state. One look at his face and my heart is stunned. Now, after hearing their conversation, the mind is in shock as well.

Who knows what all must be happening in his brain! A spell of stillness has assailed mine. Often in the night, the din of saan-saan rings and hisses in my ears and I'm unable to sleep. Does the cacophony and guttural bellowing of cattle continuously ring in his ears, too? Day and night it must bell and toll, ringing and ringing. We needlessly blame a man who is ill. My brother, he thinks no end of himself; or perhaps he doesn't; who knows what he thinks! He went to the extent of declaring that if our Brotherji dies it will make no difference to him. But now if he is found, we must get him treated. In all of this, my wife has had a major role to play. It was her implorations that pushed me to go and look for him. The instant she got the news she had talked me into it. Speeding up the motorcycle, we had then arrived in Lambde.

On travelling further we realised that the Sikhs had blocked the road. They weren't allowing any traffic to pass through. 'Satnam Waheguru!...Satnam Waheguru! Satnam Waheguru!...Satnam Waheguru!' Someone had insulted the sacred *Guru Granth Sahib*. Road jammed! The police were advising people to turn back. My mind had begun to hiss and fume phoon-phoon. My wife had quietly placed her hand on my mouth. Thereafter I lost count of how many villages we had driven and detoured through in order to bring brother-in-law here.

'How long has he been in this state?', the doctor asked, looking at me.

'Ji, about two months. More so since the last one week. Extremely poor...could not invest in care... His family people were saying perhaps he is addicted to bhang. Keeps chewing dry bhang all the time. His dryness seems to have increased. Rest of the circumstances are right here before you.' I had uttered a whole bunch of lies. Though one must not lie to a doctor. Sister had stated that since the last six–seven years, he had been up to all sorts of weird things, acting weird. More so since the last two years. And now at last he has reached this state. But I had uttered complete lies.

Now whatever the consequences, we shall see.

'He doesn't get violent, does he? I mean, does he hit or bash up anyone? How much anger does he express?' The doctor directs an analytical gaze towards brother-in-law. And before I can interject, he adds, 'Do not hurl stones at any one, okay! Do not throw cuss-words at any one!'

'Yes, Doctor Sahibji! They are all very good people. Very decent sorts, the sorts who labour hard to raise their kids. They never tell anyone full or half-baked things. Nor do they get into fisticuffs with people. They are great people. Very fine people!' I felt my words would motivate him, give him courage. But who knows what effect they actually had on the doctor. Perhaps some hurdle might crop up in the treatment. My heart skipped a beat. No, not in front of him. I cannot possibly tell the doctor that he becomes violent. Even now as we were bringing him here, we alone know how...!

'He will have to be admitted. You get a case-paper prepared from outside. Then we shall see what the reality is.'

'Ji, all right.' I set off to get a case-paper made. I didn't know how much money would be required for the medicines. Who would stay at the hospital? No one from the village is going to come. Nor can his small children stay here. This being a government hospital, more care would be required. Besides, in the department of mental disease, drug traders may be found to be doing even brisker business; here the pill is easily got, drugs as well. We ourselves will have to keep a watch. No woman could possibly stay here. Bloody hell, forget outsiders, even the *policeya* guarding the hospital ward could not be trusted! I fail to understand how within two minutes he had managed to build an acquaintance with my wife, and pushed off! I got angry with her—bloody, with every other fellow she starts talking without inhibition! It is because of this habit that all our family secrets are bloody broadcast to the wide world! These women have no bloody sense!

Stream of fire

Now, did you take note of this: it has been a whole month; has anyone come to ask after him? No one! Doesn't father know that his son-in-law is in the hospital since a month? Bloody money has become all and everything! Has the younger one come? Is he not his brother-in-law, too?

Bhabhi, his wife, had come, and left him some love in a hundred rupee note. Doesn't she know that a month's hospital expense is not just hundred rupees? Doesn't father know how many bundles of rupees are being incurred as expense? This is his daughter, isn't she? The mother died, so they simply abandoned her, poor that she is... And now for the past whole month, you, my wife, have been cooking for four persons and serving tea! They could have at least sent someone to help you. Doesn't father ever think of where I will get the money from? I am a lone earner here with bloody six mouths to feed! You used to say that Buddhi keeps taunting them, that she even gave a piece of her mind to Didi, who was already upset and left feeling even more upset. But I tell you, it is good what she did. Now Didi, too, will go and tell her father that so much money is being spent, and also who has been spending it! My tolerance has collapsed. I wish to take leave of the doctor. I wish that they take him home and continue with his treatment from there. The hospital expenses are too steep.

'Why do you lose heart? *Dil chhotta kyun karde ho, ji?* Thank the Lord that he has recovered and is well. You know what state Brotherji was in. Now he is cured ninety per cent. Doctor Sahib was saying he will be relieved in two or three days. Don't you lose your composure now. As for the family folks, these are matters of personal discretion. We did not do this for them. We have done this for Didi. She, poor thing, has never seen any comfort in her life. Now just because they have all abandoned him does not mean that we will, too. You don't worry. Money is the soil of one's hands. It keeps coming and going. You do one thing, go visit some hill station for a couple of days. I shall raise the money for you. Your soul will feel soothed... The hospital we will manage among ourselves. Now Brotherji is quite well and conscious. He showers his blessings upon you constantly. Didi, too, had uttered your name and become emotional. Remembering her mother, she says, this brother of mine does not let me feel the lack of my mother. Just think for yourself, she must be blessing you so much from the bottom of her heart-soul and bones. Come on now, get up, have your breakfast, and off you go—and go via the hospital!' The wife's tenor sounded weepy. But she has regained her composure.

'What you say is right, but I'm unable to tolerate certain matters anymore... Those buggers keep darting acerbic arrows into my chest at one time or the other...!'

'I did say, didn't I, that we are not doing anything for their sake. We are doing it all for Didi's sake. Come on, get up now, you're getting late!'

She...I honestly don't know what she is made of. It is difficult to understand my wife. Right now she is a goddess of compassion. But when it comes to her own kin, she becomes a cannonball of fire! Can neither figure her out, nor can I tolerate the grief of my sister. Well, the Supreme Lord has done us well, for sure.

Come Khusro, let's head home

Well, never mind, one must work with a wee bit of patience. It seems she is now involved with another. Besides she is an unmarried girl. Better to keep eye on a prospect where marriage can also be arranged. Moreover, she herself had divulged the matters of her heart. But why does my heart still fret over her? Day and night my thoughts anchor around her and spin incessantly. Neither work nor shirk. All the time before my eyes, just her. Even in dreams, just her. But some patience is also required. A breakup will surely follow. How girls are these days we all know...!

'Yaar, she lives with someone else. I know everything...!'

'You know nothing! She has had a breakup... Now she is with no one. Earlier she was with me. Then we had a breakup. Then she got involved with some other person... Now their breakup, too, is underway. Now she is with me only. You know nothing, son. So don't you worry!'

These two are getting petrol filled. I have no idea who they are, but just look at the conversation they are having! Have they got wind of what goes on in my heart? No, no. They are talking about their own concerns. Look at the boy, how smooth he is; yolks union and breakup in the same breath. Is it as smooth really? No. The tension on his face reveals the boil that is rising within him. That which is in his heart he is unable to express. That is something else. No, he cannot be such a *badbola*, a blabbermouth, that is. Lo, I speak his name, and the badbola himself appears right before my eyes! Now I will be compelled to listen to his tales! He is a comrade. Whatever comes to his mouth, he blurts out. Even though you might not wish to listen, you will for you must. These days he is bitten by the bug called terrorism in Punjab, over which he constantly obsesses. Here, listen:

'...Now all those who were later given one *murbha* of land, that is, about twenty-five acres, those people had left from here. They had carried the burden of their *chakkis* upon their backs. A chakki in those days was a slab of stone used for grinding grain. They laboured there. For two generations, therefore, they were able to become owners of land. When they got uprooted and migrated here, the land they got in exchange was arid and fallow. They that had lived prosperous lives over there were driven to days of beggary and hardship over here. Those that came and settled in Jalandhar, they, too, were given arid land. ...Even those that were given lands in Kapurthala. How they used to moan as they tilled the sand, sowing peanuts. What used to happen? The crop would just not grow. Then tube wells were introduced. Electricity came. Now you know that earlier, during the time of the *Angrez*, the Sikhs had rebelled. Well, what did the Angrez do thereafter? They did two things straightaway. The first thing was that they strengthened the Bisat Do-aab Canal. So that the Sikhs who were from Majha...the Majha Sikhs were at that time even more radical and defiant; the ones who had waged battles with Maharaja Ranjit Singh, they were from Majha. Well, if only they would move away from Majha and do farming—they were farmers by origin—prosperity would have dawned on them and swung them the other way. The Angrez did not build the border; they drew it on the other side. Then they carved other canals through the Punjab. These were canals that had been laid earlier in the eighteenth century. Once these canals were laid, the waters reached far and wide. This enabled people to prosper and save some money.

'Then there was the *lagaan*, revenue that used to be collected during the time of the Mughals and during Ranjit Singh's reign as well. The army used to collect the revenue. People would resist the payment of lagaan. So the wealthy village folk plus the officials of the revenue department—the *tulkedar*, the *lambardar* or village head, and the welfare officer—would get together and accompanied by the army, they would go to the villagers and demand, give us lagaan, give! If they refused to pay, they would be punished. Often the poor folks would borrow money from the village *sahukar* to pay their share of the lagaan. If nobody paid, they were all punished. A wooden plank was hung around the offender's neck. This same procedure was followed during the times of Ranjit Singh as well...

'...civil rule the British had come and established. Judiciary was separated. Powers were taken away from the *tehsildars* or executive magistrates of the district. They had the powers to make arrests, but only arrests concerning revenue defaulters. If someone did not pay revenue, he was thrown into a 'revenue jail'. But in these jails they could not keep anyone for more than a month. The food expenses of the inmates would also fall on the tehsildar's head. Therefore, the two were separated. Thereafter, in place of the army, the lagaan began to be collected by the lambardar. There was no interference from the police; the tehsildar used to manage it all. The *hawalat* or prisons had been built in the tehsil itself. The defaulters would be brought, tied up with ropes, and thrown in! But a fortnight or a month later, they had to be released. Meaning, this was the upper limit. Which means that until Maharaja Ranjit Singh's times, there was army rule. Civil rule was brought in by the English.

'That is why people regarded the English as better rulers. They brought development. They brought the railways, the telegram. They established hospitals, a few shaggy schools, too, at the district board level. They established harmony. Law was implemented with strict discipline. Dare the *thanedar* be slack or lax if a murder was reported in his area! Why would he not nab the culprits? The thanedar would go to the villages and set up camp there. Then he would search. Only after the culprits were caught would he plan a return. Not like now when even the writing of the F.I.R. is delayed. The English established a civil raj. They gave us civil administration. Then, when people began to demand freedom and turned against the state, then they quashed them. And they divided them, too. They divided the Indian nation. They said that Hindustan will become too big an empire to rule. Therefore let us break it up. Make a replica of it so in case they haggle or bicker, we can push them to war with it. That is why Pakistan has continued to receive weapons for free. They strengthened their armed forces. Centuries went past. Then there was the uproar between Amrica and Birtannia. Take the case of getting Liyaquat Ali killed. ...In the end again Birtannia was compelled to bow down. In comparison to Amrica, where is it now, big brother...!'

Look here, this one will neither stop nor go silent or relent. Let me therefore vamoose from here.

(Dear reader, here if you wish to acquaint yourself with the thoughts of the Comrade, then you could look up 'Comrade's prattle'.)

Light your cigar from my heart, love

Today the mind is ever so slightly in its place. Sister's visage is blooming, too. There is alacrity in her limbs. My brother-in-law has been relieved from the hospital. Sister hastily gathers her belongings, returns things taken from here and there, showers blessings.

'Okay *beta*, now you obey your mother's instructions. Don't take to addiction again. See how hard she has struggled to get you treated. Don't trouble her anymore now! Okay Brotherji, you take care of your health. Keep this bottle of water; it will be of use to you. Don't know how many days you will have to stay. God does good to all. Did we have any hope of his recovery? An entire month passed by. But the Lord heeded our pleas. May all be well with my brothers. May their children live and prosper. If they had not held our hand, who knows what might have happened...my heart-soul trembles at the thought. Now, if he stabilises, how very blessed it will be...!' She succumbed to her emotions.

'Come now, sister, stop this...wrap up the act! After dropping you off, I've got to report for work as well!' I do not wish to see her crying.

'...Yes, yes, we will go. It's been a month. We had these people's immense support. At odd hours of the night his wife was always beside me. He, too, kept a constant vigil. On the one hand, there's illness and sorrow; on the other hand, if someone speaks even two words of kindness and love, half the sorrow is gone. We drew such immense strength from them. Come, let's get going, brother... This bedding, please take it back. The children did not spread it on the floor—hundred illnesses thrive in hospitals! Take care of my children!'

This one has gone berserk. Anyway, it is good that she, too, has breathed a few breaths of solace. And now her temper is going to rise...that same *khadoos* doctor has arrived. Amazing! She doesn't get ruffled even by him. In fact, she has herself ushered him this way.

'Doctor Sahib, *namaste*! You have done a lot of good for us poor people. May *Rabb* grant wellbeing to your children. May they prosper. The entrails of a poor soul bless them!'

What I am wondering is if this poor soul has ever peeped into her own inner self? No, it seems. Never. I don't think so. This madcap here, even him she addresses with the same love and devotion! Yaar, these women are a very dedicated lot. The way they do *mohabbat*, even Rabb must be jealous! I cannot do such mohabbat with anyone. Whereas in women, I don't know what kind of fire it is that burns in them. Now just see the mohabbat she has for this mad fellow—it is her love which has made him recover. Otherwise there was no hope. Not due to correct treatment, but due to love and blessings he has recovered.

Well, now why don't they carry on home by themselves? Besides, the three of us will be uncomfortable on the motorcycle. And besides, I've got to go to office as well. Right then, let me tell them... Let them just catch a tempo from here and reach home.

That shouldn't be too hard...it's not as if they have to press and carry oil! He is well now. He can go live in his home.

'You people can take a tempo from here. Here, take the fare. So brother, your life has now improved. Take care of your children now and go about your work. Now the treatment is over. Next time, nobody will provide support. Now you manage by yourselves. And do continue to take the medicines!'

Many days later, having come to buy medicines, today sister had come home. And she gave us such stitches in our sides with hilarious caricatures of her mothers-in-law! Made us roll with laughter! Once she begins, she is simply amazing. Said, 'One person asked, Brotherji, how come there aren't any bones in the fish? So another responded, you may remove your shoe and eat it!'

When I inquired after brother-in-law, sister said, 'He is all right now. He does not do any drugs now. One day he had gone out for a day's labour. Got exhausted. So we suggested that he stay home and stitch footballs. Now he does one or two *khoppe* a day. One *khoppa* makes half-a-football shell. But drugs he does not do anymore. Yes, sometimes he smokes a *beedi.*'

Well, I said, that he cannot give up. Never mind. That much is okay...

And I had kept gazing into her eyes for a long time—they were so clear and free of falsehood.

Glossary and notes

> 'Bharat—Hindustan—that class uses these words only. These words are born from their social background. Comrade speaks from schooling. Pagal from experience. Professor from his intellect...the Communists live in constant fear of the government, the state...their socio-political sensibility and how the Hindu cultural hegemony still grips them... These words Bharat/Hindustan come out of their lips unconsciously...the invisible traces that underlie their consciousness....I am a *shahdai*—when I write, I go really deep. I keenly study the character—the dynamics, the nails, how many times he blinks his eyes, his language, ideology, context etc....how the language lets in the contexts.'
>
> —Des Raj Kali

Ambedkari: a follower of Dr Ambedkar.

Angrez: the English or the British.

antar-atma: deep inner consciousness; spirit-soul.

atank-vadi: terrorist.

atam manthan: soul-searching, introspection; literally, a churning of the soul.

Awadhi: one who lives in the city of Awadh; also the language spoken in the region.

badbola: a blabber-mouth.

Bahujan Samaj Party: the third largest national political party in India, it was founded by Kanshi Ram in 1984 to represent the *bahujans* (literally, meaning 'people in majority'), or people from the Scheduled Castes and Scheduled Tribes (OBCs) as well as religious minorities that together comprise 85 per cent of India's population but are still divided into 6,000 different castes. The party draws inspiration from the philosophy of B. R. Ambedkar, Mahatma Jyotiba Phule, Narayana Guru, Periyar E. V. Ramaswamy and Chhatrapati Shahuji Maharaj. Kanshi Ram named his protégée Mayawati as his successor in 2001.

Baisakhi (*Vaisakhi*): the harvest festival of the Punjab region; the Punjabi new year falls on the first day of *Vaisakh* which is the first solar month of the Punjabi calendar, Khalsa Sirjana Divas, which marks the birth of the Khalsa in the year 1699 and the Mesha Sankranti festival. It is celebrated on either 13 or 14 April.

Bajrangbali: another name for Hanuman, son of the Hindu wind god Pawan, and a devotee of Lord Ram.

balaa: someone or something that is bothersome or troublesome.

bal brahmachari: a child celibate; Hanuman is also known as one.

bawasir: piles, constipation or haemorrhoids.

beedi: a small, thin cigarette made of tobacco hand-rolled in *tendu* leaf.

besura: singing that is out of tune; also a person who sings out of tune.

beta: son.

bhabhi: brother's wife; sister-in-law; also used to formally address the wife of a friend, colleague or stranger.

bhagat: holy man.

bhai: brother.

bhang: marijuana.

bhangra: a traditional Punjabi folk dance.

bhet: devotional hymns sung in praise of a deity.

bijjoo: a small rodent found in Punjab; also used to refer to a foolish person.

Bisat Do-aab canal: the canal passing through the Doab region between rivers Sutlej and Beas. '*Do aab*' literally means water of two rivers.

brahminvad: brahminism.

buddhi: old woman, hag.

buddhi rooh: ancient spirit, spirit of a hag.

buddhu: fool, nincompoop.

chaaih: mother or grandmother in the Jhangi dialect of Punjabi.

chacha: father's younger brother.

chachi: fraternal aunt; father's younger brother's wife.

chakki: flour-mill made of two heavy, round, flat slabs of stone used for grinding grain.

Chandi-like: the Hindu goddess Chandi, known for her rage and destructive power, is the fiercest form of goddess Parvati, Lord Shiva's consort.

chaubara: traditional Punjabi houses often had two floors—ground floor and first floor; the room on the first floor with windows on all four sides was known as a *chaubara*.

chetna: consciousness; presence of mind.

chhotta dewar: husband's younger brother; younger brother-in-law.

chirag: earthen lamp with a cotton wick immersed in oil.

Chuhras, Chamars and Valmikis: Chuhras or Churas are a community who have been compelled to scavenge as a caste occupation. The Chamars are a caste of tanners. The Valmikis are a Dalit community who have historically faced exclusion and oppression in Indian society and are frequently victims of anti-Dalit violence by members of other castes. The Valmikis claim to have originally descended from Valmiki, who is credited with having written the epic *Ramayana*. Following the example of B. R. Ambedkar, the Valmikis have turned away from Hinduism to avoid the persecution associated with Hindu caste practices.

dadi: paternal grandmother.

dadi-sas: fraternal grandmother-in-law, that is, the mother-in-law of one's own mother-in-law!

dadree: a skin infection that erupts in a cluster of blisters.

darvesh: a Sufi saint, mendicant or dervish; a member of a Muslim, specifically Sufi, religious order who has taken vows of poverty and austerity. The *darvesh* have a saying about anger management: if a person is in the grip of anger, they should try to reduce their weight from 40 kilos to 12 grams.

desh: country

desi: indigenous, country-made.

dhalaan: a shamanic cure or ritual to ward off or protect against black magic.

dhalaa-ee: a metalsmith, one who smelts, shapes and works with metal.

dhrupad: see shastriya sangeet.

didi: elder sister; also a generic way of respectfully addressing any woman older than oneself.

dukh: grief, suffering.

dupatta: a large, long scarf or stole of doubled cloth draped across the shoulders as part of traditional women's dress in Punjab, north India, and the subcontinent.

durdasha: misfortune.

gadholi: an embroidered patchwork quilt, also called *godadi*.

gehena: ornament.

gharwali: wife; literally, the keeper of the house.

ghuman: a unit of land; eight parts of a *kanal* makes one ghuman of land.

gopis: village damsels, the reference here being to the *gopis* with whom the young Lord Krishna would dance and play *raas-leela*.

guggal, luban and *mushakpoor*: *guggal* is a fragrant resin used as incense which has purifying properties and is said to drive away evil energies, *luban* is the Urdu term for frankincense, and *mushakpoor* is a fragrant herb with anti-neurologic properties.

Guru Granth Sahib: the sacred text of the Sikhs and Sikhism.

Hakkam-Pirs: our so-called sages patronised by the State.

hawalat: prison.

Hudd hi ho gayi: a proverb, meaning this is the very limit (of the matter).

hukam: order.

hukkah (*hookah*): a pot with an extended pipe used for smoking tobacco; tobacco is placed in a bowl and heated with burning charcoal, producing smoke that is drawn through a pot of water that cools it and then into a long tube with an attached mouthpiece. A *hukki* is a small hukkah.

hukumat: governance.

Intakaal Araaji Act: a law formulated in the year 1900, it is also known as the Punjab Land Alienation Act, 1900. It was introduced by the British and put a curb on land purchase whereby it became impossible for the poor and the Dalit communities to purchase land. This Act was later reverted by the intervention of Dr Babasaheb Ambedkar.

Isabgol: psyllium husk packaged under the brand name Isabgol, it is popularly used in India to bring relief from constipation and regulate the bowels. It is usually taken at night mixed in a glass of warm water or warm milk.

jagirdar: land-owning feudal lords; literally, owner of a *jagir* or piece of land.

jaikara: the ritual shouting of religious slogans in a collective voice.

Jan Sangh: The Bharatiya Jan Sangh, popularly known as Jan Sangh, an Indian political party that existed between 1951 and 1977.

jeth: husband's elder brother, brother-in-law.

ji: suffix used to denote respect when added to names, titles of persons, kinship terms, places, even inanimate objects; when used alone, it also means yes or affirmation.

jijaji: sister's husband.

junoon: an Urdu word, it refers to a state of madness, obsession or passion for an issue, person or thing.

kanjar: a mule; one who is mule-like; a pimp; a caste known for pushing its daughters into prostitution; also used as a word of abuse.

karkhana: a workshop or manufacturing unit.

karuna rasa: the aesthetic representation of the emotion of sadness or grief.

kasba: a suburban township.

kavi darbar: an assembly of poets.

kendriya satta: power at the centre or *kendra*; central government.

khadanwan: wooden slippers, often worn by sages and holy men as a mark of austerity.

khadoos: stubborn; adamant; rude.

khasra number: a portion of land, the area of which is separately entered under an indicative number in the record of land ownership rights; the number allotted to a land or property by the revenue department upon its purchase. Cultivated land is classified into seven types. The register of crop inspection is called *khasra girdawari*.

khatri: a Punjabi variant for the kshatriya caste.

khich-khich pich-pich: constant and repeated argument and bickering.

khoppa: half of a football shell, often stitched by the poor as a means of earning.

kila: a measure of 4,840 square yards of land, approximately an acre.

kothri: a hovel or humble dwelling, typically of poor people.

Krishna *Leela*: Lord Krishna's divine play or *leela* in this world.

kulbul-kulbul: the seething, wriggling movement of a cluster of worms or insects.

kutcha: makeshift, unfinished, being in a crude or raw state.

lagaan: land revenue.

lakkad-dada: great-great grandfather.

lambardar: (*numbardar*) an important and powerful official of the governing body of a village or town who is invested with wide-ranging governmental powers, including revenue collection and maintaining law and order in the village; a state-privileged status, *lambardari* was usually bestowed as a hereditary title on wealthy *zamindar* or land-owning families in villages and towns across India and Pakistan.

Lataji: a reference to Lata Mangeshkar, a famous and popular Indian playback singer, also known by her fans as 'The Nightingale of Bollywood'.

mahal: palace.

Majha Sikhs: Majha is the region between rivers Beas and Ravi in Punjab. Sikhs who live in the region are called Majha Sikhs.

mama: maternal uncle, mother's brother.

mami: maternal aunt, wife of one's mother's brother.

manoor: a defect formed in inappropriately baked or overbaked bricks; a defective and discarded brick.

Marasi: (Mirasi) a low-caste, itinerant community of singers, musicians and performers who earn by entertaining and amusing people at marriages, festivals and social functions.

marlaa: a unit of land containing 30 and 1/4th square yards, a measure that is equal to the twentieth part of a *kanal*.

masar: maternal uncle, husband of one's mother's sister.

masat: a sage or a saint.

masi: maternal aunt, mother's sister.

mazaar: the grave of a *pir* or Sufi saint.

mistry: mason.

mohabbat: love.

mohalla: neighbourhood, locality.

moora: a shirker, lazybones.

mujaare: peasants, farm hands also known as *haari*.

mullak (*mulk*): one's country or native place.

murbha: a unit of land measuring about 25 acres. The region beyond river Ravi in West Punjab was uncultivated terrain. Large tracts of this land, in *murbhas*, were given free to farmers for cultivation.

napunsak: impotent, useless.

nar natak: human drama.

parav: book, episode, section or chapter.

pardhan: chief or leader of a social unit or organisation.

pbaaji: brother.

peeng: a swing made of cloth or rope and slung from tree branches, mostly in villages. The *peeng* which Radha and Krishna share in 'She, I and Space' has been translated as a 'rope swing'. To convey the intimacy of sharing a peeng, which enlists for a more intimate proximity than is conveyed by the word 'swing', it would not suffice to use 'hammock'.

phatakree (*phitkari*): alum.

phoon-phoon: onomatopoeic words expressing the release of pressured air from the nostrils.

phupharji: fraternal uncle, husband of one's father's sister.

Pingalwala's charity: charity in the name of the indigenous Sufi of Pingalwal.

pir-fakir: the name given in Punjabi/Urdu to a Muslim saint or holy man. Pir, literally, 'old/wise (person)', is a common title for a Sufi saint or master who guides and instructs his disciples on the Sufi path.

Pirzada: the Sufi Pirs.

policeya: a colloquial manner of referring to a policeman.

Poona Pact: an agreement between B. R. Ambedkar and Mahatma Gandhi on behalf of the depressed classes and caste Hindu leaders on the reservation of electoral seats for the depressed classes in the legislature of the British India government. It was made on 24 September 1932 at Yerwada Central Jail in Poona (now Pune), India. The pact was signed by Ambedkar on behalf of the depressed classes and by Madan Mohan Malviya on behalf of the caste Hindus as a means to end the fast that Gandhi undertook in jail as a protest against British Prime Minister Ramsay MacDonald's decision to give separate electorates to depressed classes for the election of members of provincial legislative assemblies in British India.

poonjipati: capitalist; a wealthy person.

pranali: a system or line of functioning.

raas-leela: *raas* is a form of folk dance performed in a huge circle; also another name for Krishna leela.

Rabb: God.

'*Raghupati Raghava Raja Ram*': sometimes called '*Ram Dhun*', it is a popular *bhajan*, or devotional song, which was a favourite of Mahatma Gandhi. The lyrics were taken from the original Hindu text *Shri Nama Ramayanam* written by Lakshmanacharya.

raj: rule; government.

rajniti: politics.

raj-tantar (*rajtantra*): structure of governance.

rajai (*razai*): comforter, two-layered quilt with cotton stuffing.

randi (*rand*): prostitute; also an abuse word.

riyasat: land that belongs to the king or ruler..

riyaz: daily practice and honing of one's craft or skill, especially by a singer, poet or artist.

rooh: a spirit, soul.

rotti: round flatbread made from wholewheat flour.

saalam tonga: tonga hired for a one-way ride.

saeen: title used by a sage or a saint, meaning godfather.

sahukar: moneylender.

sala: wife's brother, brother-in-law; also commonly used as an abuse.

sali: wife's younger sister.

sansar: world, existence.

sarkar: government; power; authority; a highly-placed and powerful government officer.

sarpanch: elected head of the village *panchayat* or governing body.

satta: power.

shaktishali: powerful, strong.

sharab: liquor.

shastriya sangeet: Hindustani classical music. *Dhrupad* is an ancient lyrical genre based on a *raga*, and the oldest of major vocal styles associated with Hindustani classical music and also related to the South Indian Carnatic tradition. It is best sung by one with a powerful voice as it is rendered vigorously to swift beats.

Shiromani Gurudwara Prabandhak Committee (SGPC): an organisation of Indian Sikhs responsible for the management of *gurdwaras*, Sikh places of worship in the states of Punjab, Haryana, Himachal Pradesh and the Union Territory of Chandigarh. The SGPC is governed by the chief minister of Punjab. It manages the security, finances, facility maintenance and religious aspects of the gurdwaras as well as the upkeep of archaeologically rare and sacred artifacts, including weapons, clothes, books and writings of the Sikh Gurus.

shenta: a wooden staff with rubber attached to one end.

sindoor: vermillion powder, traditionally worn in the parting of the hair by married Hindu women as a symbol of wedlock.

skrruch-skrruch: the sound of slippers being dragged along while walking.

suba-states: *suba* means province; here it refers to the Punjabi Suba states which held a majority of Punjab's populace. The Punjabi Suba was formed in the 1950s following the Punjabi Suba movement.

talkhee: mild.

tamasha: (here in context) histrionics. A dramatic spectacle of tangled egos and emotions, in its original sense, the *tamasha* is a folk performing art.

tantar (*tantra*): structure.

tarr-tarr: onomatopoeic expression suggesting mindless nonsensical prattle.

taya: fraternal uncle, father's elder brother; *tayi* is the wife of *taya*.

taziya: in India and South Asia, a replica of the tomb of Husain, the martyred grandson of Prophet Muhammad, that is carried in processions during the festival of Muharram.

tehsil: sub-district, an administrative and revenue unit about one-third of the district area; there would be two to three tehsils in a district.

tehsildar: executive magistrate of a tehsil; also a tax officer.

thanedar: police officer in charge of a *thana* or police station; a sub-inspector.

tuhni: fumigation.

tulkedar: (*taluqdar*) a revenue department official responsible for the collection of taxes in colonial times.

tunn-tunn: the sound of a bell or gong.

Tussi kirpa karo: You kindly bless us.

udarikaran: liberalisation.

ugg diyaan ptaal: hocus-pocus, nonsense.

Valmikis: see note on Chuhras and Chamars.

vidaee: the ceremony of leave-taking as a new bride leaves her parental home for her husband's home.

yaar: friend, buddy; also lover.

Writings from the soil of wounds

A mulaquat with Des Raj Kali*

Neeti Singh: Please talk about your birth as a writer. Also throw some light on your sources of inspiration—a philosophical creed, book or person.

Des Raj Kali: In actual terms, my birth as a writer happened during my days in college. Prior to that, I had begun to string together a few short stories; however, the thought that they should be sent for publishing or that I could become a writer hadn't surfaced as yet. I was then a student of DAV College, Jalandhar. In those days, a few Punjabi writers had begun to surface. They in turn were in touch with other prominent and established writers, and would often organise writer's meets around them. I, too, got introduced to the writerly circles. There were Devinder Mand, Bhagwant Rasoolpuri, Surinder Sohal, who were among the better Punjabi writers. The senior writers whom I got to know included Prem Gorkhi, whose name used to feature on top. Around that time, a story of mine was published in the monthly journal *Naagmani*, which was produced under the editorship of Amrita Pritam. That was my moment of *balle-balle*! (He grins.) And I became a writer.

But I know this, that behind my emergence as a writer lies a lot that is very unusual, that is unique. There is a lot that is

*This interview of the author by Neeti Singh, in Vadodara, Gujarat, September 2016, was first published as 'Desraj Kali: Meditations on the Roots, Soil and Soul of Writing', on gatewaylitfest.com, 12 September 2017. It is edited and published here with the kind permission of Mohan Kakanadan, Director, Gateway LitFest. The interview, originally conducted in Punjabi, was translated by Neeti Singh.

unspoken, a lot of undertones and resonant notes. There is a substantial amount of cultural history. There are marriage songs or *ghodiyan*,[1] there are *suhags*[2] and there are *keerne*[3] or songs of lamentations as well. Foremost among them all is the generic *kissa-kaav*[4] that my father, Bapaji, used to read out to us in a singsong way, which had begun to sprout as a literary seedling through my childhood years. Bapaji would also read and sing to us the *Heer* of Waris Shah, Pandit Kishorchand Bandewal's *Jaani Chor* in twelve parts, the lore of *Nal Damayanti*, *Roop Basant*, *Zindagi Bilas*, *Shah Baheram*, *Haatam-tai*, and dozens of other such narratives. We children would listen. The village elders, too, would flock to listen to these ballads and *kissas* from him. The ballads in the Punjabi kissa-kaav tradition are incredibly powerful and evocative, and their historical scope is immensely rich. Punjabi vocabulary itself is a veritable treasure house.

In our village there is a shrine of Pir Zinda Shah. Every year, an *uras* or a commemoration is hosted there. There was a saint who used to come there to sing with his *tumba*.[5] An amazing Sufi atmosphere he would engender. He, too, was my inspiration. Then the homes that were located behind ours used to worship Gugga Pir. Every year they would feed the followers of Gugga Pir. The Gugga singers would perform the *Katha* all through the night. The Katha was most engrossing; in it one would find interesting anecdotes and details of Baba Gorakhnath's life and his impact on his followers. All these tales, this music, this richness, this immense passion that suffused the atmosphere around me became my inspiration. This becomes apparent in my novels as well.

Along with this, my father's guru, Sant Pritamdas Chishti Sabri, was a Sufi. Prior to him, Sarvar Sarkar Sant Brahmadasji of Phillor had been his guru. We used to visit their *dargahs*[6] where *qawwalis*[7] used to be performed. These experiences touched my being and initiated me into the Sufi ethos. Similarly my uncle, Chacha Joginder Das, had taken as his guru one Nath Lahuka Dasji. He would arrive riding a black mare. He would insist on sitting on a *takhatposh*.[8] He would don a *langot*,[9] and no other garment besides. On one shoulder would be a typical cotton sling bag, called *bugli* in Punjabi, and in one hand he would carry a *bairagan.*[10] Many a time, my own heart would be tempted to follow in his footsteps and don that peculiar garb. Even now there are times that I am tempted. Like Nath Lahuka Das, there used to live in our neighbourhood an elder called Lachman Das. He would perform the *phanda*, a voodoo ritual performed with peacock feathers on ailing people. People used to call him *chela* or disciple. Lachman Das's guru was a Nath of the village Madulli Bahmana and was also known as Sant Kadeanwale. I acknowledge the influence of all these gurus and *pirs* in my childhood. These are the very seeds, the very roots of my *itihas*.

Singh: Would you like to comment on the emotional as well as the conceptual source that drives you to write? What is the emotion that drives you to function as a creative, thinking Dalit novelist and public figure?

Kali: I cannot hope to answer this question in its entirety. However, there was something at heart, something that cannot be defined, though one could certainly talk around it. My first story that was published in *Naagmani* was titled, 'A Streak of Light'. This story is about a Dalit woman of my village who was extremely poor. A woman from the mountains, she was incredibly beautiful. Her husband was a useless idler, utterly foolish. He would do no work at all. This woman used to work in the house of a police officer of our village. The village people would often link her name with the police officer, but only behind her back. Once, however, during a game of cards, someone from among the wise men of the village addressed this woman in a sarcastic tone, while alluding to the same police officer. And this resolute woman blew a gasket in turn. She grabbed an iron sickle and charged at him. Her anger was worth watching. From that sickle raised to hit, I had sensed the genesis of a sliver of light. I felt I should write about it. Then, as I mentioned, some families that lived behind our house used to feed *tolis* or bands of the followers of Gugga Fakir.[11] Among them, one family was extremely poor. My father and mother, although they were poor themselves, often used to help them. The feet of that man got infected with *karoheea*, a fungal disease contracted from long and continuous exposure to dirty water. He had no money for medical treatment. I saw that the big toe of his foot eventually rotted and fell off. That the body parts of a human being should just break and fall off was sheer injustice. I was deeply affected by it and I wrote about it. These people were my very own people, from my own milieu. I had grown up in their very hands. Their sorrows were weird, extremely bizarre and phenomenally huge. The shrieks of their wounds continued to walk around in some nook of my consciousness. That is why I have written about them. Now the times have changed. People, too, have changed. However, the shadows of these people continue to linger on my soul, which is reflected in my writings. The shrieks of those wounds have turned me into a writer.

Singh: How did the idea and form of *Shanti Parav* evolve?

Kali: *Shanti Parav* the novel came to me in fits and starts. I was in search of the Self. And I was excavating, digging under the skin of my context, my history and surroundings. At the same time I was trying to comprehend the psyche of the people who dwelt around me. I was trying to configure the human that was withering away in the scope of things. I was also making an attempt to comprehend the functioning of the state, state politics, and rigorously researching the social, cultural subtexts therein. I had been observing how near impossible it was to separate the Indian from the influence of his/her classical past. Whichever caste or creed s/he might belong to. Therefore, my characters were being shaped in a melting pot that was multi-dimensional and multi-layered. That is when I felt that beneath their construction simmered much that was invisible but was intense in its impact. Then I took in hand the three characters of the under-text, and through their agency I explored the reasons that lay beneath their manifest constructions. An attempt was also made to make this work novel in terms of its craftsmanship, and to ensure that the experiment employed herein was adequately justified.

I work extremely hard on my novels. I work on them for years. My work showcases the historicity of cultural behaviour. At the same time it exposes the practice of branding and isolating segments of marginalised people. It also holds up a mirror to the churning human currents of our times. They appear fictional despite being otherwise. They are the fruit and soil of my thought process and also of my politics. In the matrix of literature, they also reflect my ideological stance.

Singh: What are your views on the '*Shanti Parva*' of the *Mahabharata* as a text? How do you relate to it as a subaltern who might himself have been a soldier lying slain upon the blood-drenched battlefield of Kurukshetra?

Kali: The discourse that sits under the title of '*Shanti Parva*' in the *Mahabharata* is an extremely significant one. I have combed through classical literature and while researching this particular *Parva*, I noticed that in all manner of appearance this treatise was penned in the aftermath of war during a period of peace which, rationally speaking, should have induced calm reflection and introspection on the reasons that caused the battle. But, contrary to expectation, the '*Shanti Parva*' merely justifies the great war. It was in fact an enterprise of the brahmins and the elite classes to condone that which was a terrible blunder, and to mask in the guise of divine dictate and righteous action all those actions that had plundered and pulled to shreds human life and dignity. Then again, most thoughts in the '*Shanti Parva*' were ascribed to Draupadi alone. This amounted to rendering worthless the blood of all those soldiers who were martyred in battle. The entire treatise essentially proffered to justify the monarch's pathetic atrocities over his people. Conceptually opposed to this brand of ideology, I said to myself, the 'Shanti Parav' that I will write shall reflect on the so-called times of peace that followed on the heels of Bharat's battle for independence, and therein I shall perform an analysis of that period and will ensure that the scale of truth is heavier. The old '*Shanti Parva*' had its own philosophy; my *Shanti Parav* will have another. Through this novel I have dealt that twelfth book of the *Mahabharata* a philosophical rebuttal. It is a combat at every level—at the level of literary genre as well as the level of philosophy.

Singh: In the book, in the upper half of the text, you speak of mainstream discourses like dominion, capital, political will, corruption, terrorism and state violence. In the upper-text, however, where aspects of human existence on the margins is played out through fiction, these ideological influences do not reflect. Also there seems to be a slight disconnect. The monologues in the under-text span a huge chunk of detail from the Indian past, ending in the early years post-Independence, whereas the characters that people the stories in the upper-text seem to belong to a more recent past or more recent times—they have laptops and go on long drives, features typical of the late twentieth and early twenty-first century. Please explain.

Kali: Let me clarify. The mainstream discourses that prevail, their impact cannot be gauged upfront. Their impact is not the kind where one hits another on the head and they both end up injured and soaked in blood. The lash of their whip is soundless, long-drawn and slow. The other aspect of my writing is that it is not about *yatharth* or reality but about the echo of that *yatharth*. It is that which is awakened in my heart as a response to that reality. About the probable *yatharth*, about that which was born in the mind-heart—good/bad, political/non-political, that is what my literature is about. I do not present the probable as truth; that is why my writing sometimes verges on the absurd. That which is realistic touches upon the breath of my thoughts, becomes sharper in the process and emerges forth as writing. That is why the mainstream discourses that are presented in the novel are functional; they only operate from behind the scenes, they are invisible and cannot be seen upfront. That is why I said that if my characters are to be understood, then the discourse below—the under-text—has to be understood. The under-text is instrumental, it is key to decoding the narrative above, the upper-text, though this is not immediately apparent. All that history, all that past, all those dealings in the present, they are instrumental in fashioning the behaviour of my characters, which I have discussed in the under-text through the agency of the three old characters. For instance, when one of them claims that our legacy is colonial, examining the characters in the upper-text through that lens and framework will provide clarity in perceiving the dynamics of their general behaviour. The two narratives are therefore deeply imbricated with one another.

To further refine and clarify the conceptual aspect, I believe no event that transpires in the world around us transpires in isolation. All, all of us are connected. I cannot claim that my current behaviour as it exists today and the age of the *Mahabharata* in my past are disconnected. They are very much connected. When we uproot a blade of grass, god knows how many lakh convulsions must seize Mother Nature in their grip. And even to create or give birth to that single blade of grass we do not know the number of agencies that are employed and consumed in the process. Similar is the functioning of the political scenario. That is why all the manipulations of time, the fashionings and sculptings of history, the *darshan* and the *sahitya*, all these enter a state of coalition and they walk. The present has with the future an alliance or a coalition. That is why the under-text in my *Shanti Parav* feeds the nature and behaviour of the characters in the upper-text in a terribly intense interaction. This needs and calls for some delicate attention on the part of the reader.

Singh: Tell us about your fascination with names and characters from Indian mythology. Many of your novels are informed by a sensibility dyed in the history, myth and grandeur of knowledge-traditions from the Indian past.

Kali: If you wish to understand the Bharatiya individual, from any perspective—be it from his/her spiritual context, or socio-cultural context, or even in terms of his/her political associations—you cannot hope to do so by separating the Indian people from Indian mythology. For an understanding of the Bharatiya *manukh*, it is essential to understand the body of Bharatiya myth. The Indian denizen is born in myth and also dies in myth. This is what my research has revealed. Whenever I have tried to understand a character, its roots, I have found, one way or another, lie in some myth. Therefore, myth is a very significant part of my sahitya.

Even to understand my politics you need to have knowledge of Indian myths and mythical lore.

The title of my first novel is *Parneshwari*. This mythical character descended into my consciousness during my readings of Nath, Buddhist and Charvaka Sahitya.[12] The next novel, titled *Pratham Pauran*, too, is the result of my engagement with the classical texts. *Antaheen*, another novel, carries in its thought process a similar context. The connection of *Shanti Parav* to mythology is more obvious. In my stories, too, you will encounter Indian mythology and a virtual historical tour of Bharat. This could be the fallout of my intellectual engagement, my *vichar-dhara*, and also my politics. One more thing, the wisdom that is to be found in Bharatiya mythology, the wealth of words and stories there are and the manoeuvrings of narration are limitless and unfathomable. For a writer, therefore, the reading of mythology is most essential. Many litterateurs of Punjabi and literary critics try to escape from it; that is why they do not reach the bottom of it. Perhaps.

Singh: Please share with us your definition of 'violence' in brief.

Kali: In my understanding, violence that is invisible is far more intense than violence that is visible. In Punjab we have a saying: caste, creed or discrimination cannot be gauged—that, I believe, is the reason why its sting is even sharper. Violence has always been perpetrated over the women and Dalits of Bharat. In *Shanti Parav*, I have tried to explore several dimensions of this aspect of violence.

Singh: Are you a capitalist, a communist, or neither of the two?

Kali: I do not hold capitalist thoughts and neither am I a communist. The rising curve of capital we cannot turn. It's a natural phenomenon. Human society is bound to evolve; besides there is so much contained in it that the natural, unnatural or inhuman will coexist. I stand with the thought process that blind consumption, unthinking consumerism is inhuman; we cannot save ourselves from it. There are of course many more dimensions to this. However, when a human is debased in any manner, I stand in opposition and in resistance to it.

Singh: What is your idea of a perfect society, and whether it is at all possible? For even if equations were to change, the underdog and the bully will always be a part of our worlds.

Kali: There is no word like 'perfect' in my understanding. There are crores and crores of varieties of all sorts of people and circumstances mired with all kinds of complexities; all kinds of contexts are there and thriving disputes; some matter sits well with one, while with another it does not. Each individual has his or her own justification, his or her own logic. Therefore, nothing can ever be perfect or complete. Nor should it ever be. The affluent and powerful are bound to dominate. But I always say that struggle or resistance, the *sangharsh* for equality must persist through all time. Even where it is not apparent, they are prevalent, they prevail endlessly. A person may not even be aware of it, yet s/he continues unconsciously to put up a resistance.

I often speak about the names in my family's nomenclature. My father's name is Niranjan Das, my Biji's name is Prakash, my elder sister is Simro, my elder brother is Satnam—all these names, they are of the Nirguna (Bhakti) *parampara*. They have been carrying on a philosophical tradition from generation to generation. This, too, is a form of resistance. A tug of war between Saguna and Nirguna thought cultures. Perhaps no one is consciously aware of it, but the battle prevails.

Singh: A utopia in Kali's words would be?

Kali: I feel that we writing people, whichever society we dream of is a utopia in itself. Between social probability and the dreams that we dream there is a huge gap. This has always been there. We, however, are people of a positive outlook, and therefore, we cannot stop dreaming.

Singh: The male characters in your novel are submissive and passive as compared to their female counterparts who come across as more vocal and assertive, even though both genders exist within shared contexts of poverty, victimisation and victim psychology. Please comment.

Kali: This is a very discerning question, indeed. I have said this earlier as well that whenever I look at all that goes on around me, at any incident or character or society at large, when I do examine them, I do so with a certain keenness and depth. I travel into its past and present at great length. A lot of effort goes into the exercise. Our *tabla*,[13] the percussion instrument, has two drums: one is male while the other is female. According to the rationale of the *Ardhanareshwar*,[14] the male tabla, which is the *vadak* or the player, is kept on the left side while the female tabla is kept on the right, so that the emotion can be articulated and manifested. It has been observed that the female side of the tabla requires a lot of effort from the artist; tuning and aligning it to the *shadaj* or *pancham*[15] notes is a challenging task. If this side is not in tune then there is no pleasure in the performance. Through this same lens I have also seen society at large, seen the female and male characters. That is the reason you will find that my women characters will be in better rhythm, in better harmony. And this is a fact of natural law, also a fact of social law. This is a very sensitive aspect, natural as well as societal, towards which insufficient attention has been drawn. Nature has created woman in her primary aspect; that is why she is *janani*—motherhood incarnate. And as she is the nurturing agency, she is bound to be more cruel as well, for she must protect herself in every possible manner and ensure that she flourishes. I have seen that there is more self-control in a woman. Another very significant aspect is that compared to women in general, the Dalit woman is more independent and assertive, in social terms as well as in terms of culture. The women who are around me are more dominating as compared to others. This is a *samajik*, a social truth that I have witnessed, experienced and written about.

Singh: And finally, for whom do you write? Who are the readers of your fiction? And have they changed in the course of these years from when you wrote your first novel to now, your recent one, the sixth?

Kali: Many of my friends tell me that my writing is not for the casual reader. I, too, agree with that. To fully comprehend my writing, a lot of mental acrobatics must be applied. However, despite that, there is a readership for my kind of writing. At times, it has been my experience that the reader comes up with interpretations that have been beyond one's conscious grasp, though subconsciously they have been a part of one's mindscape. It is true that along with the writer, the reader, too, undergoes a transformation and that with the passage of time the reader's comprehension also changes and evolves; his/her perception, too, becomes clearer and sharper. Secondly, my literature has been better received by the newer generation of readers as compared to those who tend to view it from stereotypical contexts or perspectives. Readership that was attached to Punjabi literature of the earlier canon was much troubled by my writings, but newer readers have welcomed it. The new reader of Punjabi literature is advancing at a swift pace. This, too, can be ascribed to contemporary social dynamics.

Notes

1. *ghodiyan*: pre-wedding songs sung at the groom's house.
2. *suhag*: pre-wedding songs sung at the bride's house.
3. *keerne*: elegiac songs of lamentation, sung on someone's passing away.
4. *kissa-kaav*: a literary tradition of narrative poetry recounting tales of valour, love and heroism, it hails from oral storytelling traditions that came into Punjabi from Persian and Arabic poetic traditions, for example, the tales of Heer-Ranjha and Sohni-Mahiwal. For details, see Sant Singh Sekhon and Kartar Singh Duggal, *A History of Punjabi Literature* (New Delhi: Sahitya Akademi, 1992).
5. *tumba*: a string instrument made out of a small gourd that is locally grown in Punjab.
6. *dargah*: a shrine built over the grave of a revered religious figure, often a Sufi saint or darvesh. It holds great importance for the followers of Sufism.
7. *qawwali*: a form of Sufi Islamic devotional music originating in the Indian subcontinent, and notably popular in the Punjab and Sindh regions of Pakistan, parts of North India, and Bangladesh. Nusrat Fateh Ali Khan, Sabri Brothers, Abida Parveen, Fareed Ayyaz and Abu Muhammad are some of its famous exponents.

8. *takhatposh*: among certain *fakir* traditions in northern India, it is the norm of austerity to sit or sleep on a bed of hard wood. Sitting on a plank of wood also symbolises to the mystic his or her nearness to nature.

9. *langot*: a loincloth worn by men, typically made of cotton or muslin.

10. *bairagan*: a short thick staff carried by *sadhus* and fakirs, it has a triangular or t-shaped top on which to rest the elbow while meditating, thus helping the mystic to maintain a comfortable, upright posture while meditating.

11. Gugga Fakir: also known as Gogaji Pir or Jahar Veer Gogga, he is a folk deity and a famous mystic revered by both Muslims and Hindus, especially those of the lower caste, and worshipped in some northern states of India, especially Rajasthan, Haryana, Uttarakhand, Punjab and Uttar Pradesh. Known as Gugga Fakir or Gugga Pir in the Punjab region, he is worshipped as a warrior, a hero of the region, and venerated as a saint and also as a snake god.

12. Charvaka Sahitya: also known as Lokayata, Charvaka is an ancient school of Indian materialism which holds direct perception, empiricism and conditional inference as the proper and authentic sources of knowledge, embraces philosophical scepticism and rejects the Vedas, Vedic ritualism and supernaturalism. The Charvakas were anti-brahminical and believed in the efficacy of four (not five) elements, comprising earth, water, wind and fire (minus sky). Known as a heterodox school of Indian philosophy, history recounts that the Charvakas or Lokayatas were burnt alive, so also their literature. For more details, see Debiprasad Chattopadhyaya, *Lokayata: A Study of Ancient Indian Materialism* (New Delhi: People's Publishing House, 1959).

13. *tabla*: an Indian percussion instrument comprising twin drums used as an accompaniment to Indian classical and mainstream vocal and instrumental music performances.

14. *Ardhanareshwar*: a composite androgynous form of Lord Shiva and his consort Parvati (also known as Devi, Shakti and Uma in this icon) depicted as half male and half female, split down the middle. The right half is usually the male Shiva. Ardhanareshwar represents the synthesis of masculine and feminine energies of the universe (Purusha and Prakriti) and illustrates how Shakti, the female principle of God, is inseparable from (or, according to some interpretations, the same as) Shiva, the male principle. The union of these two principles is exalted as the root and womb of all creation. Another view is that Ardhanareshwar is a symbol of Shiva's all-pervasive nature.

15. *shadaj* and *pancham*: the first and the fifth, respectively, of the seven notes of the musical scale in Indian classical music.